# Selected Poems
## of Sir Charles G. D. Roberts

Ὦ φίλε πάν, τε καὶ ἄλλοι ὅσοι τῇδε θεοί,
δοίητε μοὶ καλῷ γενέσθαι τἄνδοθεν.

British Library Cataloguing-in-Publication Data
A catalogue record for this book is available from the
British Library

# Charles G. D. Roberts

Charles G. D. Roberts was born on 10th January 1860, in Douglas, New Brunswick, Canada. He was the eldest of the six children of Emma Wetmore Bliss and Rev. George Goodridge Roberts (an Anglican Priest).

The family moved to Fredericton in 1873 where the young Roberts attended Fredericton Collegiate School. The headmaster, George Robert Parkin, inspired Roberts to love classical literature and introduced him to the poetry of Dante Gabriel Rossetti and Algernon Charles Swinburne. He went on to study at the University of New Brunswick, earning his B.A. in 1879 and an M.A. in 1881. On the completion of his education, Roberts remained in New Brunswick and took the position of principal at Chatham High School, a role he held between 1879 and 1881. He followed this with a further two years as principal at York Street School, Fredericton, before moving to Toronto to edit Goldwin Smith's magazine *The Week*.

Roberts married Mary Fenety in 1880, with whom he had five children. In the same year he also published his first collection of poetry *Orion and Other Poems*. This work received favourable reviews and established him as a promising Canadian literary figure. During his time as a professor at University of King's College, Nova Scotia, Roberts published his second book of poetry, *In Divers Tones* (1886).

In 1895, a request for a leave of absence was turned down and he decided to resign from his university post to become a full-time author. The following year he published his first novel *The Forge in the Forest* (1896). Roberts's most successful literary genre was that of the animal story which featured in works such as *Earth's Enigmas* (1896) and *Eyes of the Wilderness* (1933). He also wrote romance novels and several non-fiction works on Canada.

Roberts left his family in 1897 to move to New York to work as an editor for *The Illustrated American*. He remained in New York for ten years until he decided to cross the Atlantic. He spent the next 18 years living in Paris, London, and Munich.

Roberts returned to Canada in 1925. He settled there and remarried in 1943 at the age of 83, but died soon after. His funeral was held in Toronto, but his ashes were returned to Fredericton, where he was interred in Forest Hill Cemetery.

Charles G. D. Roberts

# PREFATORY NOTE

IN this volume of selections my ten books of verse, from "Orion and Other Poems," 1880, to "The Iceberg and Other Poems" published in 1934, are all represented. But the selections are not arranged chronologically. It has seemed to me advisable to classify them in some cases according to their form—as Odes, Ballads, Sonnets—and in other cases according to their subject matter. I have departed from this arrangement, however, in the case of "The Iceberg and Other Poems," which volume I am here reprinting as a whole, because it has hitherto appeared only in a limited *de luxe* edition.

In making my selections I have sought to show the whole range of my work in verse, from the earliest derivative stuff, such as the "Ode to Drowsihood" and the extracts from "Orion," written in my teens, up to "Westcock Hill" which was written just in time to get into my 1934 volume. In the division "Odes" I have placed "Ave" (1892), with its severe classicism of technique, near the "Ode for Canada's Diamond Jubilee" (1927), with its subjective approach and its essentially modern looseness of structure. From early youth to the present day I have always been alive to the moment, keenly aware of contemporary currents of thought, action and emotion. There is a vast change to be noted between the rigid Ovidian elegiac metre of the "Tantramar Revisited" and the "Pipes of Pan" (1887), with their formal alternation of hexameter and pentameter lines, and, on the other hand, the freedom of structure of "The

Iceberg," the interstanzaic fluidity of line of "The Squatter" (1934). I am far from claiming that this change is of necessity growth. But it is divergence, and as such might, I think, be taken into account in any serious evaluation of my verse which the critic may find it worth while to make.

As there is just now a good deal of difference of opinion—a healthy difference, if at times somewhat acrimoniously expressed—in regard to what constitutes poetry both in form and in content, it may not be unfitting for me to indicate my own position in the matter. The following sentences from a Preface by Mr. Humbert Wolfe seem to me relevant:

"There is no such thing" (as modern verse) "and never has been. Nor is there ancient verse. There are only oldish men in each generation misunderstanding what is being written now, side by side with youngish men misunderstanding what was written then. Verse itself cares nothing for the oldish men nor the youngish men, nor indeed for anything but itself."

It seems to me it is all a matter of the succeeding cycles of reaction. Reaction is life. The more healthy and vigorous the reaction, the more inevitably does it froth up into excess. The excess dies away of its own violence. But the freshness of thought or of technique that supplied the urge to the reaction remains and is clarified, ultimately to be worked into the tissue of permanent art.

C. G. D. R.

THE ERNESCLIFFE,
*October 31,*
*1936.*

# CONTENTS

IX

## IV. POEMS PHILOSOPHICAL AND MYSTICAL

# I. The Iceberg and Other Poems

# SELECTED POEMS

## The Iceberg

I was spawned from the glacier,
A thousand miles due north
Beyond Cape Chidley;
And the spawning,
When my vast, wallowing bulk went under,
Emerged and heaved aloft,
Shaking down cataracts from its rocking sides,
With mountainous surge and thunder
Outraged the silence of the Arctic sea.

Before I was thrust forth
A thousand years I crept,
Crawling, crawling, crawling irresistibly,
Hid in the blue womb of the eternal ice,
While under me the tortured rock
Groaned,
And over me the immeasurable desolation slept.

Under the pallid dawning
Of the lidless Arctic day
Forever no life stirred.
No wing of bird—
Of ghostly owl low winnowing
Or fleet-winged ptarmigan fleeing the pounce of death,—
No foot of backward-glancing fox
Half glimpsed, and vanishing like a breath,—
No lean and gauntly stalking bear,
Stalking his prey.
Only the white sun, circling the white sky.
Only the wind screaming perpetually.

And then the night—
The long night, naked, high over the roof of the world,
Where time seemed frozen in the cold of space,—

[ 3 ]

Now black, and torn with cry
Of unseen voices where the storm raged by,
Now radiant with spectral light
As the vault of heaven split wide
To let the flaming Polar cohorts through,
And close ranked spears of gold and blue,
Thin scarlet and thin green,
Hurtled and clashed across the sphere
And hissed in sibilant whisperings,
And died.
And then the stark moon, swinging low,
Silver, indifferent, serene,
Over the sheeted snow.

But now, an Alp afloat,
In seizure of the surreptitious tide,
Began my long drift south to a remote
And unimagined doom.
Scornful of storm,
Unjarred by thunderous buffeting of seas,
Shearing the giant floes aside,
Ploughing the wide-flung ice-fields in a spume
That smoked far up my ponderous flanks,
Onward I fared,
My ice-blue pinnacles rendering back the sun
In darts of sharp radiance;
My bases fathoms deep in the dark profound.

And now around me
Life and the frigid waters all aswarm.
The smooth wave creamed
With tiny capelin and the small pale squid,—
So pale the light struck through them.
Gulls and gannets screamed
Over the feast, and gorged themselves, and rose,
A clamour of weaving wings, and hid
Momently my face.
The great bull whales
With cavernous jaws agape,
Scooped in the spoil, and slept,
Their humped forms just awash, and rocking softly,—
Or sounded down, down to the deeps, and nosed
Along my ribbed and sunken roots,
And in the green gloom scattered the pasturing cod.

[ 4 ]

And so I voyaged on, down the dim parallels,
Convoyed by fields
Of countless calving seals
Mild-featured, innocent-eyed, and unforeknowing
The doom of the red flenching knives.
I passed the storm-racked gate
Of Hudson Strait,
And savage Chidley where the warring tides
In white wrath seethe forever.
Down along the sounding shore
Of iron-fanged, many-watered Labrador
Slow weeks I shaped my course, and saw
Dark Mokkowic and dark Napiskawa,
And came at last off lone Belle Isle, the bane
Of ships and snare of bergs.
Here, by the deep conflicting currents drawn,
I hung,
And swung,
The inland voices Gulfward calling me
To ground amid my peers on the alien strand
And roam no more.
But then an off-shore wind,
A great wind fraught with fate,
Caught me and pressed me back,
And I resumed my solitary way.

Slowly I bore
South-east by bastioned Bauld,
And passed the sentinel light far-beaming late
Along the liners' track,
And slanted out Atlanticwards, until
Above the treacherous swaths of fog
Faded from the view the loom of Newfoundland.

Beautiful, ethereal
In the blue sparkle of the gleaming day,
A soaring miracle
Of white immensity,
I was the cynosure of passing ships
That wondered and were gone,
Their wreathed smoke trailing them beyond the verge.
And when in the night they passed—
The night of stars and calm,
Forged up and passed, with churning surge

[ 5 ]

And throb of huge propellers, and long-drawn
Luminous wake behind,
And sharp, small lights in rows,
I lay a ghost of menace chill and still,
A shape pearl-pale and monstrous, off to leeward,
Blurring the dim horizon line.

Day dragged on day,
And then came fog,
By noon, blind-white,
And in the night
Black-thick and smothering the sight.
Folded therein I waited,
Waited I knew not what
And heeded not,
Greatly incurious and unconcerned.
I heard the small waves lapping along my base,
Lipping and whispering, lisping with bated breath
A casual expectancy of death.
I heard remote
The deep, far carrying note
Blown from the hoarse and hollow throat
Of some lone tanker groping on her course.
Louder and louder rose the sound
In deepening diapason, then passed on,
Diminishing, and dying,—
And silence closed around.
And in the silence came again
Those stealthy voices,
That whispering of death.

And then I heard
The thud of screws approaching.
Near and more near,
Louder and yet more loud,
Through the thick dark I heard it,—
The rush and hiss of waters as she ploughed
Head on, unseen, unseeing,
Toward where I stood across her path, invisible.
And then a startled blare
Of horror close re-echoing,—a glare
Of sudden, stabbing searchlights
That but obscurely pierced the gloom;
And there
I towered, a dim immensity of doom.

[ 6 ]

       A roar
Of tortured waters as the giant screws,
Reversed, thundered full steam astern.
Yet forward still she drew, until,
Slow answering desperate helm,
She swerved, and all her broadside came in view,
Crawling beneath me;
And for a moment I saw faces, blanched,
Stiffly agape, turned upward, and wild eyes
Astare; and one long, quavering cry went up
As a submerged horn gored her through and through,
Ripping her beam wide open;
And sullenly she listed, till her funnels
Crashed on my steep,
And men sprang, stumbling, for the boats.

But now, my deep foundations
Mined by those warmer seas, the hour had come
When I must change.
Slowly I leaned above her,
Slowly at first, then faster,
And icy fragments rained upon her decks.
Then my enormous mass descended on her,
A falling mountain, all obliterating,—
And the confusion of thin, wailing cries,
The Babel of shouts and prayers
And shriek of steam escaping
Suddenly died.
And I rolled over,
Wallowing,
And once more came to rest,
My long hid bases heaved up high in air.

       And now, from fogs emerging,
I traversed blander seas,
Forgot the fogs, the scourging
Of sleet-whipped gales, forgot
My austere origin, my tremendous birth,
My journeyings, and that last cataclysm
Of overwhelming ruin.
My squat, pale, alien bulk
Basked in the ambient sheen;
And all about me, league on league outspread,
A gulf of indigo and green.

[ 7 ]

I laughed in the light waves laced with white,—
Nor knew
How swiftly shrank my girth
Under their sly caresses, how the breath
Of that soft wind sucked up my strength, nor how
The sweet, insidious fingers of the sun
Their stealthy depredations wrought upon me.

Slowly now
I drifted, dreaming.
I saw the flying-fish
With silver gleaming
Flash from the peacock-bosomed wave
And flicker through an arc of sunlit air
Back to their element, desperate to elude
The jaws of the pursuing albacore.

Day after day
I swung in the unhasting tide.
Sometimes I saw the dolphin folk at play,
Their lithe sides iridescent-dyed,
Unheeding in their speed
That long grey wraith,
The shark that followed hungering beneath.
Sometimes I saw a school
Of porpoise rolling by
In ranked array,
Emerging and submerging rhythmically,
Their blunt black bodies heading all one way
Until they faded
In the horizon's dazzling line of light.
Night after night
I followed the low, large moon across the sky,
Or counted the large stars on the purple dark,
The while I wasted, wasted and took no thought,
In drowsed entrancement caught;—
Until one noon a wave washed over me,
Breathed low a sobbing sigh,
Foamed indolently, and passed on;
And then I knew my empery was gone;
As I, too, soon must go.
Nor was I ill content to have it so.

Another night
Gloomed o'er my sight,
With cloud, and flurries of warm, wild rain.
Another day,
Dawning delectably
With amber and scarlet stain,
Swept on its way,
Glowing and shimmering with heavy heat.
A lazing tuna rose
And nosed me curiously,
And shouldered me aside in brusque disdain,
So had I fallen from my high estate.
A foraging gull
Stooped over me, touched me with webbed pink feet,
And wheeled and skreeled away,
Indignant at the chill.

Last I became
A little glancing globe of cold
That slid and sparkled on the slow-pulsed swell.
And then my fragile, scintillating frame
Dissolved in ecstasy
Of many coloured light,
And I breathed up my soul into the air
And merged forever in the all-solvent sea.


## The Squatter

Round the lone clearing
Clearly the whitethroats call
Across the marge of dusk and the dewfall's coolness.

Far up in the empty
Amber and apple-green sky
A night-hawk swoops, and twangs her silver chord.

No wind's astir,
But the poplar boughs breathe softly
And the smoke of a dying brush-fire stings the air.

The spired, dark spruces
Crowd up to the snake fence, breathless,
Expectant till the rising of the moon.

[ 9 ]

In the wet alders,
Where the cold brook flows murmuring,
The red cow drinks,—the cow-bell sounds *tonk-tonk*.

*     *     *     *     *

From his cabin door
The squatter lounges forth,
Sniffs the damp air, and scans the sky for rain.

He has made his meal,—
Fat bacon, and buckwheat cakes,
And ruddy-brown molasses from Barbados.

His chores all done,
He seats himself on the door-sill,
And slowly fills his pipe, and smokes, and dreams.

He sees his axe
Leaning against the birch logs.
The fresh white chips are scattered over the yard.

He hears his old horse
Nosing the hay, in the log barn
Roofed with poles and sheathed with sheets of birch-
    bark.

Beyond the barn
He sees his buckwheat patch,
Its  pink-white  bloom  pale-gleaming  through  the
    twilight.

Its honeyed fragrance
Breathes to his nostrils, mingled
With the tang of the brush-fire smoke, thinly ascending.

Deepens the dusk.
The whitethroats are hushed; and the night-hawk
Drops down from the sky and hunts the low-flying
    night-moths.

*     *     *     *     *

The squatter is dreaming.
Vaguely he plans how, come winter,
He'll chop out another field, just over the brook.

[ 10 ]

He'll build a new barn
Next year, a barn with a haymow,
No more to leave his good hay outside in the stack.

He rises and stretches,
Goes in and closes the door,
And lights his lamp on the table beside the window.

The light shines forth.
It lights up the wide-strewn chips.
For a moment it catches the dog darting after a rabbit.

It lights up the lean face
Of the squatter as he sits reading,
Knitting his brow as he spells out a month-old paper.

  \*  \*  \*  \*  \*

Slowly the moon,
Humped, crooked, red, remote,
Rises, tangled and scrawled behind the spruce-tops.

Higher she rises,—
Grows rounder, and smaller, and white,
And sails up the empty sky high over the spruce-tops.

She washes in silver,
Illusively clear, the log barn,
The lop-sided stack by the barn, and the slumbering
  cabin.

She floods in the window,—
And the squatter stirs in his bunk,
On his mattress stuffed with green fir-tips, balsamy
  scented.

  \*  \*  \*  \*  \*

From the dark of the forest
The horned owl hoots, and is still.
Startled, the silence descends, and broods once more
  on the clearing.

[ 11 ]

## Re-birth

I had stumbled up thro' Time from the slime to the
    heights,
  Then fallen into the stillness of the tomb.
For an age I had lain in the pulseless, senseless dark,
  I had swooned in the darkness of the tomb.

I had slept for an age without a dream or stir
  Till a voice came, troubling the pools of sleep.
From the long-forgotten bones, the immemorial dust,
  I fled up from the smother of my sleep.

A naked soul, I bathed in the light ineffable,
  I floated in the ecstasy of light.
Yet I ached with desire for a dream I could not grasp,
  And I struggled to pierce beyond the light.

As the light had been a veil I swam through the veil
  And sank through shadows to a blissful gloom.
And the ache of my desire was sweetly assuaged
  As I sheathed me blindly in the gloom.

In my heart, as it seemed, I heard a craving, faint cry.
  I was darkly aware of moving warmth.
I thirsted, and my groping thirst was satisfied;
  And I slumbered, wrapt and folded in the warmth.

Once again was I snared in the kindly flesh of man.
  The kind flesh closed away my sight.
But before the mists of temporal forgetting shut me in
  I had seen, far off, the Vision and the Height.

## Westcock Hill

As I came over Westcock Hill
  My heart was full of tears.
Under the summer's pomp I heard
  The spending of the years.
*Oh, the sweet years!  The swift years!*
*The years that lapse away!*

[ 12 ]

I saw the green slopes bathed in sun,
  The marshlands stretched afar,
And, hurrying pale between its dikes,
  My memoried Tantramar.
  *Oh, the sweet years!   The swift years!*
  *The years that lapse away!*

The salt tang and the buckwheat scents
  Were on the breathing air;
And all was glad.   But I was sad
  For one who was not there.
  *Oh, the sweet years!   The swift years!*
  *The years that lapse away!*

I wandered down to Westcock Church,
  The old grey church in the wood.
Kneeling, I heard my father's voice
  In that hushed solitude.
  *Oh, the sweet years!   The swift years!*
  *The years that lapse away!*

I saw again his surpliced form.
  I heard the hymning choir.
Shadows!—and dreams!   Alone remained
  The ache of my desire.
  *Oh, the sweet years!   The swift years!*
  *The years that lapse away!*

He sleeps;—how many a year removed,
  How many a league withdrawn
From these dear woods, these turbid floods,
  These fields that front the dawn.
  *Oh, the sweet years!   The swift years!*
  *The years have lapsed away!*


## Taormina

A little tumbled city on the height,
  Basking above the cactus and the sea!
What pale, frail ghosts of memory come to-night
  And call back the forgotten years to me!
    *Taormina, Taormina,*
    *And the month of the almond blossom.*

In an old book I find a withered flower,
  And withered dreams awake to their old fire.
How far have danced your feet since that fair hour
  That brought us to the land of heart's desire!
    *Taormina, Taormina,*
    *Oh, the scent of the almond blossom.*

The grey-white monastery-garden wall
  O'erpeers the white crag, and the flung vines
      upclamber
In the white sun, and cling and seem to fall,—
  Brave bougainvilleas, purple and smoky amber.
    *Taormina, Taormina,*
    *And the month of the almond blossom.*

You caught your breath, as hand in hand we stood
  To watch the luminous peak of Aetna there
Soaring above the cloudy solitude,
  Enmeshed in the opaline Sicilian air.
    *Taormina, Taormina,*
    *Oh, the scent of the almond blossom.*

We babbled of Battos and brown Corydon,—
  Of Amaryllis coiling her dark locks,—
Of the sad-hearted satyr grieving on
  The tomb of Helicè among the rocks
    O'erhung with the almond blossom,—

Of how the goat-boy wrenched apart the vines
  That veiled the slim-limbed Chloe at her bath,
And followed her fleet-foot flight among the pines
  And caught her close, and kissed away her wrath.
    *Taormina, Taormina,*
    *And the month of the almond blossom.*

And then—you turned impetuously to me!
  We saw the blue hyacinths at our feet; and came
To the battlements, and looked down upon the sea—
  And the sea was a blue flame!

          *     *     *     *     *

The blue flame dies.   The ghosts come back to me.
    *Taormina, Taormina,*
    *Oh, the scent of the almond blossom.*

[ 14 ]

## To a Certain Mystic

Sometimes you saw what others could not see.
   Sometimes you heard what no one else could hear:—
A light beyond the unfathomable dark,
   A voice that sounded only to your ear.

And did you, voyaging the tides of vision
   In your lone shallop, steering by what star,
Catch hints of some Elysian fragrance, wafted
   On winds impalpable, from who knows how far?

And did dawn show you driftage from strange
      continents
   Of which we dream but no man surely knows,—
Some shed gold leafage from the Tree Eternal,
   Some petals of the Imperishable Rose?

And did you once, Columbus of the spirit,
   Essay the crossing of that unknown sea,
Really touch land beyond the mists of rumour
   And find new lands where they were dreamed to be?

Ah, why brought you not back the word of power,
   The charted course, the unambiguous sign,
Or even some small seed, whence we might grow
   A flower unmistakably divine?

But you came empty-handed, and your tongue
   Babbled strange tidings none could wholly trust.
And if we half believed you, it was only
   Because we would, and not because we must.

## Spirit of Beauty

Spirit of Beauty,
   Never shall you escape me.
Through glad or bitter days
   Hearten and shape me.

Since first these eyes could see
   Still have they sought you.
Since first my soul knew dream
   My dreams have wrought you.

[ 15 ]

Since first my ears were unsealed
    To the whitethroat's plaining,
Between the gusts of the wind
    And the low sky's raining,

Your voice I hear
    In the laughter of leaves, in the falling
Of waves on an empty shore
    And a far bell calling.

When I clasp a warm, dear hand
    I know you are holding me.
When I lean to the lips of my love
    Your arms are enfolding me.

And when Night comes
    And the faithless senses forsake me,
Out of my cold, last sleep
    You, you shall awake me.


## Unsaid

I thieved a skein of gossamer thread
And wove me a web of moonbeam wings,
That I might hover over your head
And dare to whisper into your dream
The lovely, disastrous, scarce-thought things
That even my eyes had left unsaid.

Under the veil of your slumbering eyes
I caught the heart of your dream by surprise.
I uncovered your dream; and found there hidden,—
Sleeping cherished though waking forbidden,—
All the disastrous, scarce-thought things,
The wonderful things I had left unsaid.


## Be Quiet, Wind

Be quiet, wind, a little while,
    And let me hear my heart.
You chiming rivulet, still your chant
    And stealthily depart.

[ 16 ]

You whisperings in the aspen leaves,
  You far-heard whip-poor-will,
You slow drop spilling from the rose—
  You, even you, be still.

I must have infinite silence now,
  Lest I should miss one word
Of all my heart would say to me—
  Now, when its deeps are stirred.

Hardly I dare my breath to draw
  Lest breathing break the spell,—
While we commune, my heart and I,
  In dreams too deep to tell.

## Presences

The shadow of the poplar
Beside my cabin door
Has trembled on the floor.
Tho' no wind walks the forest tops
Across my window sill
It trembled and was still.

The broad noon sunlight basking
On every flower and tree
Was still as light can be.
What made those withered leaves whirl up,
And drift a space, and fall—
As they had heard a call?

Why are those harebells nodding
As if an unseen wing
Had set them all aswing,
Tho' up and down the forest glade
No other blade or bough
Stirs from its slumber now?

The stillness and the brightness
Companion me.  I hear
A footfall drawing near
Tho' no sound breaks the noonday hush.
A sweet breath stirs my hair,—
But there is nothing there!

[ 17 ]

What gracious presences
Are these I cannot see
Tho' they come close to me?

\*　　\*　　\*　　\*　　\*

I think I shall have pleasant dreams
In silence charmed and deep
When I lie down to sleep.

## Pan and the Rose

Came Pan to the garden
On a golden morning,
The dew of the thickets
Adrip on his thighs.
He thrust through the hollyhocks,
Stamped the bright marigolds,
And scanned pale Dianthe
With indifferent eyes.

But aloof in the garden
He spied one blossom,
A rose but half open
To the insistent sun,—
Her petals enclosing
The dew of young ecstasy,
The perilous perfume
Of life just begun.

His hot heart pounding
In his shaggy bosom,
The tender red petals
To his lips he drew.
With aching rapture
And a wild, wild wonder,
He drained the distillage
Of that honeyed dew.

\*　　\*　　\*　　\*　　\*

And ever thereafter
He needs must wander,
Piping his lone plaint
Beside the shadowy stream,—

[ 18 ]

Nor heeds the enticing
Of white nymphs in the copses,—
His heart tormented,
And his parched lips thirsting
For the draught that assuages them
No longer save in dream.


## Bat, Bat, Come Under My Hat

*(A Modernity)*

Twelve good friends
Passed under her hat,
And devil a one of them
Knew where he was at.

Had they but known,
Then had they known all things,—
The littleness of great things,
The unmeasured immensity of small things.
They had known the *Where* and the *Why*,
The *When* and the *Wherefore*,
And how the Eternal
Conceived the Eternal, and therefore
Beginning began the Beginning;
They had apprehended
The ultimate virtue of sinning;
They had caught the whisper
That Vega vibrates to Arcturus,
Piercing the walls
Of heavy flesh that immure us.

But if they had known,
Then had there been no mystery;
And Life had been poorer,
And laughter unsurer,
And the shadow of death securer,
By lack of this brief history.

## Quebec, 1757

*(From the French of Philippe Aubert de Gaspé)*

An eagle city on her heights austere,
    Taker of tribute from the chainless flood,
She watches wave above her in the clear
    The whiteness of her banner purged with blood.

Near her grim citadel the blinding sheen
    Of her cathedral spire triumphant soars,
Rocked by the Angelus, whose peal serene
    Beats over Beaupré and the Levis shores.

Tossed in his light craft on the dancing wave,
    A stranger where he once victorious trod,
The passing Iroquois, fierce-eyed and grave,
    Frowns on the flag of France, the cross of God.

# II. Odes

# Ave!

*(An Ode for the Shelley Centenary, 1892)*

## I

O tranquil meadows, grassy Tantramar,
  Wide marshes ever washed in clearest air,
Whether beneath the sole and spectral star
  The dear severity of dawn you wear,
Or whether in the joy of ample day
  And speechless ecstasy of growing June
You lie and dream the long blue hours away
    Till nightfall comes too soon,
Or whether, naked to the unstarred night,
You strike with wondering awe my inward sight,—

## II

You know how I have loved you, how my dreams
  Go forth to you with longing, though the years
That turn not back like your returning streams
  And fain would mist the memory with tears,
Though the inexorable years deny
  My feet the fellowship of your deep grass,
O'er which, as o'er another, tenderer sky,
    Cloud phantoms drift and pass,—
You know my confident love, since first, a child,
Amid your wastes of green I wandered wild.

## III

Inconstant, eager, curious, I roamed;
  And ever your long reaches lured me on;
And ever o'er my feet your grasses foamed,
  And in my eyes your far horizons shone.
But sometimes would you (as a stillness fell
  And on my pulse you laid a soothing palm)
Instruct my ears in your most secret spell;
    And sometimes in the calm
Initiate my young and wondering eyes
Until my spirit grew more still and wise.

## IV

Purged with high thoughts and infinite desire
  I entered fearless the most holy place,
Received between my lips the secret fire,
  The breath of inspiration on my face.

[ 23 ]

But not for long these rare illumined hours,
    The deep surprise and rapture not for long.
Again I saw the common, kindly flowers,
    Again I heard the song
Of the glad bobolink, whose lyric throat
Pealed like a tangle of small bells afloat.


                        V

The pounce of mottled marsh-hawk on his prey;
    The flicker of sand-pipers in from sea
In gusty flocks that puffed and fled; the play
    Of field-mice in the vetches,—these to me
Were memorable events.  But most availed
    Your strange unquiet waters to engage
My kindred heart's companionship; nor failed
    To grant this heritage,—
That in my veins forever must abide
The urge and fluctuation of the tide.


                       VI

The mystic river whence you take your name,
    River of hubbub, raucous Tantramar,
Untamable and changeable as flame,
    It called me and compelled me from afar,
Shaping my soul with its impetuous stress.
    When in its gaping channel deep withdrawn
Its waves ran crying of the wilderness
    And winds and stars and dawn,
How I companioned them in speed sublime,
Led out a vagrant on the hills of Time!


                      VII

And when the orange flood came roaring in
    From  Fundy's  tumbling  troughs  and  tide-worn
            caves,
While red Minudie's flats were drowned with din
    And rough Chignecto's front oppugned the waves,
How blithely with the refluent foam I raced
    Inland along the radiant chasm, exploring
The green solemnity with boisterous haste;
    My pulse of joy outpouring
To visit all the creeks that twist and shine
From Beauséjour to utmost Tormentine.

## VIII

And after, when the tide was full, and stilled
  A little while the seething and the hiss,
And every tributary channel filled
  To the brim with rosy streams that swelled to kiss
The grass-roots all awash and goose-tongue wild
  And salt-sap rosemary,—then how well content
I was to rest me like a breathless child
    With play-time rapture spent,—
To lapse and loiter till the change should come
And the great floods turn seaward, roaring home.

## IX

And now, O tranquil marshes, in your vast
  Serenity of vision and of dream,
Wherethrough by every intricate vein have passed
  With joy impetuous and pain supreme
The sharp, fierce tides that chafe the shores of earth
  In endless and controlless ebb and flow,
Strangely akin you seem to him whose birth
    One hundred years ago
With fiery succour to the ranks of song
Defied the ancient gates of wrath and wrong.

## X

Like yours, O marshes, his compassionate breast,
  Wherein abode all dreams of love and peace,
Was tortured with perpetual unrest.
  Now loud with flood, now languid with release,
Now poignant with the lonely ebb, the strife
  Of tides from the salt sea of human pain
That hiss along the perilous coasts of life
    Beat in his eager brain;
But all about the tumult of his heart
Stretched the great calm of his celestial art.

## XI

Therefore with no far flight, from Tantramar
  And my still world of ecstasy, to thee,
Shelley, to thee I turn, the avatar
  Of Song, Love, Dream, Desire, and Liberty;

[ 25 ]

To thee I turn with reverent hands of prayer
  And lips that fain would ease my heart of praise,
Whom chief of all whose brows prophetic wear
    The pure and sacred bays
I worship, and have worshipped since the hour
When first I felt thy bright and chainless power.

XII

About thy sheltered cradle in the green
  Untroubled groves of Sussex, brooded forms
That to the mother's eye remained unseen,—
  Terrors and ardours, passionate hopes, and storms
Of fierce retributive fury, such as jarred
  Ancient and sceptred creeds, and cast down kings,
And oft the holy cause of Freedom marred
    With lust of meaner things,
With guiltless blood, and many a frenzied crime
Dared in the face of unforgetful Time.

XIII

The star that burns on revolution smote
  Wild heats and change on thine ascendant sphere,
Whose influence thereafter seemed to float
  Through many a strange eclipse of wrath and fear,
Dimming awhile the radiance of thy love.
  But still supreme in thy nativity,
All dark, invidious aspects far above,
    Beamed one clear orb for thee,—
The star whose ministrations just and strong
Controlled the tireless flight of Dante's song.

XIV

With how august contrition, and what tears
  Of penitential, unavailing shame,
Thy venerable foster-mother hears
  The sons of song impeach her ancient name,
Because in one rash hour of anger blind
  She thrust thee forth in exile, and thy feet
Too soon to earth's wild outer ways consigned,—
    Far from her well-loved seat,
Far from her studious halls and storied towers
And weedy Isis winding through his flowers.

[ 26 ]

## XV

And thou, thenceforth the breathless child of change,
 Thine own Alastor, on an endless quest
Of unimagined loveliness didst range,
 Urged ever by the soul's divine unrest.
Of that high quest and that unrest divine
 Thy first immortal music thou didst make,
Inwrought with fairy Alp, and Reuss, and Rhine,
 And phantom seas that break
In soundless foam along the shores of Time,
Prisoned in thine imperishable rhyme.

## XVI

Thyself the lark melodious in mid-heaven;
 Thyself the Protean shape of chainless cloud,
Pregnant with elemental fire, and driven
 Through deeps of quivering light, and darkness loud
With tempest, yet beneficent as prayer;
 Thyself the wild west wind, relentless strewing
The withered leaves of custom on the air,
 And through the wreck pursuing
O'er lovelier Arnos, more imperial Romes,
Thy radiant visions to their viewless homes.

## XVII

And when thy mightiest creation thou
 Wert fain to body forth,—the dauntless form,
The all-enduring, all-forgiving brow
 Of the great Titan, flinchless in the storm
Of pangs unspeakable and nameless hates,
 Yet rent by all the wrongs and woes of men,
And triumphing in his pain, that so their fates
 Might be assuaged,—oh then
Out of that vast compassionate heart of thine
Thou wert constrained to shape the dream benign.

## XVIII

—O Baths of Caracalla, arches clad
 In such transcendent rhapsodies of green
That one might guess the sprites of spring were glad
 For your majestic ruin, yours the scene,

The illuminating air of sense and thought;
  And yours the enchanted light, O skies of Rome,
Where the giant vision into form was wrought;
  Beneath your blazing dome
The intensest song our language ever knew
Beat up exhaustless to the blinding blue!—


XIX

The domes of Pisa and her towers superb,
  The myrtles and the ilexes that sigh
O'er San Giuliano, where no jars disturb
  The lonely aziola's evening cry,
The Serchio's sun-kissed waters,—these conspired
  With Plato's theme occult, with Dante's calm
Rapture of mystic love, and so inspired
  Thy soul's espousal psalm,
A strain of such elect and pure intent
It breathes of a diviner element.


XX

Thou on whose lips the word of Love became
  A rapt evangel to assuage all wrong,
Not Love alone, but the austerer name
  Of Death engaged the splendours of thy song.
The luminous grief, the spacious consolation
  Of thy supreme lament, that mourned for him
Too early haled to that still habitation
  Beneath the grass-roots dim,—
Where his faint limbs and pain-o'erwearied heart
Of all earth's loveliness became a part,


XXI

But where, thou sayest, himself would not abide,—
  Thy solemn incommunicable joy
Announcing Adonais has not died,
  Attesting death to free but not destroy,
All this was as thy swan-song mystical.
  Even while the note serene was on thy tongue
Thin grew the veil of the Invisible,
  The white sword nearer swung,—
And in the sudden wisdom of thy rest
Thou knewest all thou hadst but dimly guessed.

[ 28 ]

## XXII

Lament, Lerici, mourn for the world's loss!
  Mourn that pure light of song extinct at noon!
Ye waves of Spezzia that shine and toss
  Repent that sacred flame you quenched too soon!
Mourn, Mediterranean waters, mourn
  In affluent purple down your golden shore!
Such strains as his, whose voice you stilled in scorn,
  Our ears may greet no more,
Unless at last to that far sphere we climb
Where he completes the wonder of his rhyme!

## XXIII

How like a cloud she fled, thy fateful bark,
  From eyes that watched to hearts that waited, till
Up from the ocean roared the tempest dark—
  And the wild heart Love waited for was still!
Hither and thither in the slow, soft tide,
  Rolled seaward, shoreward, sands and wandering
    shells
And shifting weeds thy fellows, thou didst hide
  Remote from all farewells,
Nor felt the sun, nor heard the fleeting rain,
Nor heeded Casa Magni's quenchless pain.

## XXIV

*Thou* heedest not?   Nay, for it was not thou,
  That blind, mute clay relinquished by the waves
Reluctantly at last, and slumbering now
  In one of kind earth's most compassionate graves!
Not thou, not thou,—for thou wert in the light
  Of the Unspeakable, where time is not.
Thou sawest those tears; but in thy perfect sight
  And thy eternal thought
Were they not even now all wiped away
In the reunion of the infinite day!

## XXV

There face to face thou sawest the living God
  And worshippedst, beholding Him the same
Adored on earth as Love, the same whose rod
  Thou hadst endured as Life, whose secret name

Thou now didst learn, the healing name of Death.
    In that unroutable profound of peace,
Beyond experience of pulse and breath,
    Beyond the last release
Of longing, rose to greet thee all the lords
Of Thought, with consummation in their words:


### XXVI

He of the seven cities claimed, whose eyes,
    Though blind, saw gods and heroes, and the fall
Of Ilium, and many alien skies,
    And Circe's Isle; and he whom mortals call
The Thunderous, who sang the Titan bound
    As thou the Titan victor; the benign
Spirit of Plato; Job; and Judah's crowned
    Singer and seer divine;
Omar; the Tuscan; Milton, vast and strong;
And Shakespeare, captain of the host of Song.


### XXVII

Back from the underworld of whelming change
    To the wide-glittering beach thy body came;
And thou didst contemplate with wonder strange
    And curious regard thy kindred flame,
Fed sweet with frankincense and wine and salt,
    With fierce purgation search thee, soon resolving
Thee to the elements of the airy vault
    And the far spheres revolving,
The common waters, the familiar woods,
And the great hills' inviolate solitudes.


### XXVIII

Thy close companions there officiated
    With solemn mourning and with mindful tears,—
The pained, imperious wanderer unmated
    Who voiced the wrath of those rebellious years;
Trelawney, lion-limbed and high of heart;
    And he, that gentlest sage and friend most true,
Whom Adonais loved.   With these bore part
    One grieving ghost, that flew
Hither and thither through the smoke unstirred
In wailing semblance of a wild white bird.

## XXIX

O heart of fire, that fire might not consume,
  Forever glad the world because of thee;
Because of thee forever eyes illume
  A more enchanted earth, a lovelier sea!
O poignant voice of the desire of life,
  Piercing our lethargy, because thy call
Aroused our spirits to a nobler strife
  Where base and sordid fall,
Forever past the conflict and the pain
More clearly beams the goal we shall attain!

## XXX

And now once more, O marshes, back to you
  From whatsoever wanderings, near or far,
To you I turn with joy forever new,
  To you, O sovereign vasts of Tantramar!
Your tides are at the full.   Your wizard flood,
  With every tribute stream and brimming creek,
Ponders, possessor of the utmost good,
  With no more left to seek,—
But the hour wanes and passes; and once more
Resounds the ebb with destiny in its roar.

## XXXI

So might some lord of men, whom force and fate
  And his great heart's unvanquishable power
Have thrust with storm to his supreme estate,
  Ascend by night his solitary tower
High o'er the city's lights and cries uplift.
  Silent he ponders the scrolled heaven to read
And the keen stars' conflicting message sift,
  Till the slow signs recede,
And ominously scarlet dawns afar
The day he leads his legions forth to war.

# Ode to Drowsihood

Breather of honeyed breath upon my face!
  Teller of balmy tales!  Weaver of dreams!
  Sweet conjurer of palpitating gleams
And peopled shadows trooping into place
    In purple streams
Between the drooped lid and the drowsy eye!
  Moth-winged seducer, dusky-soft and brown,
Of bubble gifts and bodiless minstrelsy
  Lavish enough!  Of rest the restful crown!
At whose behest are closed the lips that sigh,
  And weary heads lie down.

Thee, Nodding Spirit!  Magic Comforter!
  Thee, with faint mouth half speechless, I invoke,
  And straight uplooms through the dead centuries'
    smoke
The aged Druid in his robe of fur,
    Beneath the oak
Where hang uncut the paly mistletoes.
  The mistletoe dissolves to Indian willow,
Glassing its red stems in the stream that flows
  Through the broad interval.  A lazy billow
Flung from my oar lifts the long grass that grows
  To be the Naiad's pillow.

The startled meadow-hen floats off, to sink
  Into remoter shades and ferny glooms;
  The great bees drone about the thick pea-blooms;
The linkèd bubblings of the bobolink,
    With warm perfumes
From the broad-flowered wild parsnip, drown my brain;
  The grackles bicker in the alder-boughs;
The grasshoppers pipe out their thin refrain
  That with intenser heat the noon endows.
Then thy weft weakens, and I wake again
  Out of my dreamful drowse.

Ah! fetch thy poppy-baths, juices exprest
  In fervid sunshine, where the Javan palm
  Stirs, scarce awakened from its odorous calm
By the enervate wind, that sinks to rest
    Amid the balm

[ 32 ]

And sultry silence, murmuring, half asleep,
  Cool fragments of the ocean's foamy roar,
And of the surge's mighty throbs that keep
  Forever yearning up the golden shore,
Mingled with song of Nereids that leap
  Where the curled crests downpour.

Who sips thy wine may float in Baiæ's skies,
  Or flushed Maggiore's ripples, mindless made
  Of storming troubles hard to be allayed.
Who eats thy berries, for his ears and eyes
    May vineyard shade
Melt with soft Tuscan, glow with arms and lips
  Cream-white and crimson, making mock at reason.
Thy balm on brows by care uneaten drips;
  I have thy favours but I fear thy treason.
Fain would I hold thee by the dusk wing-tips
  Against a grievous season.


## An Ode for the Canadian Confederacy

Awake, my country, the hour is great with change!
  Under this gloom which yet obscures the land,
From ice-blue strait and stern Laurentian range
  To where giant peaks our western bounds command,
A deep voice stirs, vibrating in men's ears
  As if their own hearts throbbed that thunder forth,
A sound wherein who hearkens wisely hears
  The voice of the desire of this strong North,—
    This North whose heart of fire
    Yet knows not its desire
Clearly, but dreams, and murmurs in the dream.
The hour of dreams is done. Lo, on the hills the gleam!

Awake, my country, the hour of dreams is done!
  Doubt not, nor dread the greatness of thy fate.
Tho' faint souls fear the keen confronting sun,
  And fain would bid the morn of splendour wait;
Tho' dreamers, rapt in starry visions, cry
  "Lo, yon thy future, yon thy faith, thy fame!"

And stretch vain hands to stars, thy fame is nigh,
  Here in Canadian hearth, and home, and name,—
    This name which yet shall grow
    Till all the nations know
Us for a patriot people, heart and hand
Loyal to our native earth, our own Canadian land!

O strong hearts, guarding the birthright of our glory,
  Worth your best blood this heritage that ye guard!
These mighty streams resplendent with our story,
  These iron coasts by rage of seas unjarred,—
What fields of peace these bulwarks well secure!
  What vales of plenty those calm floods supply!
Shall not our love this rough, sweet land make sure,
  Her bounds preserve inviolate, though we die?
    O strong hearts of the North,
    Let flame your loyalty forth,
And put the craven and base to an open shame,
Till earth shall know the Child of Nations by her
    name!

## These Three Score Years
### (An Ode for Canada's Diamond Jubilee)

I

Oh to be back where the oatfields are blowing
  In my own Canadian home;
Where the shadows chase the shadows across the water
    meadows
  And the deep grass seethes like foam!

II

So sang the exile, wearying for dead days;
  And homeward turned o'er the long-furrowed sea
To find new wonder in the old dear ways,
  And drown in dreams fulfilled the ache of memory.

III

Deliberate Time, toiling for age on age
  To chisel one lean channel down the steep,
Or grave in stone some enigmatic page
  Of aeons lapsed in immemorial sleep,

[ 34 ]

What impulse urged you to this ecstatic haste,
    Drove you to spurn the dragging centuries,
To beat blind oafish Ignorance to her knees,
    And, in a space as brief
    To immortal eyes as that twixt bud and leaf,
To fling the marvel of a million hearths
And towered and teeming cities o'er the waste?


## IV

These three score fateful years!
    So swiftly have they sped, so fleetly wrought,
    Our eyes, confused by dust of toil and strife,
By turmoil of desires and hopes and fears,
    Have scarce perceived the miracles they wrought,
    Or sensed the splendours burgeoning into life;
Till now, on this proud day we celebrate,
    Pausing to count the cost and gain, we stand
With eyes unsealed, with wondering hearts elate,
    To view the task complete as our great Fathers
        planned.

## V

Theirs was the vision, theirs the faith far-seeing,
    And theirs the force that forged our unity,
That called a nation into instant being
    And stretched its boundaries from sea to sea.
They snared a savage continent in steel.
    They bowed the eternal icepeaks to their will.
    The clamour of old hates they bade be still.
They tamed old factions to the common weal.
And one, our poet, statesman, seer combined,
Sealed with a martyr's blood the bond his faith had
    signed.

## VI

And are we worthy these heroic sires,
    These twain world-mastering peoples whence they
        sprang?
    Doth still the breed run true,
Still in our veins upflame the ancient fires?
Make answer, Fields of Flanders, Fields of France,
    Where late our young battalions marched and sang,
    Our airmen soared the shrapnel-shattered blue!

Bear witness, Ypres and Vimy, with what cheer,
And courage clear,
And high contempt of fear,
Embattled at the grim old Lion's side,
Our scarred battalions triumphed, laughed and died!

## VII

Dying, they live imperishable, and proclaim
    Our manhood's stature to the world, their blood
A sacrament of glory, and their fame
    The enduring pledge of that new brotherhood
Of equal nations which we "Empire" name,—
That Commonwealth in which we proudly own
Love to our peers, allegiance to our Throne.

## VIII

And so I end my random song, returning
    To that which makes perchance its only worth,—
The patriot warmth within my bosom burning
    Through all my wanderings o'er the curious earth.
Friends have I found in far and alien places,
Beauty and ardour in unfamiliar faces,
But first in my heart this land I call my own!
*Canadian* am I in blood and bone!

*Read at The New Brunswick Celebration of Canada's*
*Diamond Jubilee at Fredericton.*

III. Poems of Canadian Life
and Landscape

# The Solitary Woodsman

When the grey lake-water rushes
Past the dripping alder-bushes,
    And the bodeful autumn wind
In the fir-tree weeps and hushes,—

When the air is sharply damp
Round the solitary camp,
    And the moose-bush in the thicket
Glimmers like a scarlet lamp,—

When the birches twinkle yellow,
And the cornel bunches mellow,
    And the owl across the twilight
Trumpets to his downy fellow,—

When the nut-fed chipmunks romp
Through the maples' crimson pomp,
    And the slim viburnum flushes
In the darkness of the swamp,—

When the blueberries are dead,
When the rowan clusters red,
    And the shy bear, summer-sleekened,
In the bracken makes his bed,—

On a day there comes once more
To the latched and lonely door,
    Down the wood-road striding silent,
One who has been here before.

Green spruce branches for his head,
Here he makes his simple bed,
    Couching with the sun, and rising
When the dawn is frosty red.

All day long he wanders wide
With the grey moss for his guide,
    And his lonely axe-stroke startles
The expectant forest-side.

Toward the quiet close of day
Back to camp he takes his way,
    And about his sober footsteps
Unafraid the squirrels play.

On his roof the red leaf falls,
At his door the bluejay calls,
    And he hears the wood-mice hurry
Up and down his rough log walls;

Hears the laughter of the loon
Thrill the dying afternoon;
    Hears the calling of the moose
Echo to the early moon.

And he hears the partridge drumming,
The belated hornet humming,—
    All the faint, prophetic sounds
That foretell the winter's coming.

And the wind about his eaves
Through the chilly night-wet grieves,
    And the earth's dumb patience fills him,
Fellow to the falling leaves.


## *The Logs*

In thronged procession gliding slow
The great logs sullenly seaward go.

A blind and blundering multitude
They jostle on the swollen flood,

Nor guess the inevitable fate
To greet them at the river-gate

When noiseless hours have lured them down
To the wide booms, the busy town,

The mills, the chains, the screeching jaws
Of the eviscerating saws.

Here in the murmur of the stream
Slow journeying, perchance they dream,

And hear once more their branches sigh
Far up the solitary sky,

Once more the rain-wind softly moan
Where sways the high green top alone,

Once more the inland eagle call
From the white crag that broods o'er all.

But if, beside some meadowy brink
Where flowering willows lean to drink,

Some open beach at the river bend
Where shallows in the sun extend,

They for a little would delay,
The huge tide hurries them away.

## The First Ploughing

Calls the crow from the pine-tree top
When the April air is still.
He calls to the farmer hitching his team
In the farmyard under the hill.
"Come up," he cries, "come out and come up,
For the high field's ripe to till.
Don't wait for word from the dandelion
Or leave from the daffodil."

Cheeps the flycatcher—"Here old earth
Warms up in the April sun;
And the first ephemera, wings yet wet,
From the mould creep one by one.
Under the fence where the flies frequent
Is the earliest gossamer spun.
Come up from the damp of the valley lands,
For here the winter's done."

Whistles the high-hole out of the grove
His summoning loud and clear:
"Chilly it may be down your way
But the high south field has cheer.
On the sunward side of the chestnut stump
The woodgrubs wake and appear.
Come out to your ploughing, come up to your
    ploughing,
The time for ploughing is here."

Then dips the coulter and drives the share,
And the furrows faintly steam.
The crow drifts furtively down from the pine
To follow the clanking team.
The flycatcher tumbles, the high-hole darts
In the young noon's yellow gleam;
And wholesome sweet the smell of the sod
Upturned from its winter's dream.

## The Pipers of the Pools

Pipers of the chilly pools
Pipe the April in.
Summon all the singing hosts,
All the wilding kin.

Through the cool and teeming damp
Of the twilight air
Call till all the April children
Answer everywhere.

From your cold and fluting throats
Pipe the world awake,
Pipe and mould to move again,
Pipe the sod to break.

Pipe the mating song of earth
And the fecund fire,—
Love and laughter, pang and dream,
Desire, desire, desire.

Then a wonder shall appear,
Miracle of time:
Up through root and germ and sapwood
Life shall climb, and climb.

Then the hiding things shall hear you
And the sleeping stir,
And the far-off troops of exile
Gather to confer;

Then the rain shall kiss the bud
And the sun the bee,
Till they all, the painted children,
Flower and wing get free;

And amid the shining grass
Ephemera arise;
And the windflowers in the hollow
Open starry eyes;

And delight comes in to whisper—
"Soon, soon, soon
Earth shall be but one wild blossom
Breathing to the moon!"

## In the Night Watches

When the little spent winds are at rest in the tamarack
 tree
In the still of the night,
And the moon in her waning is wan and misshapen,
And out on the lake
The loon floats in a glimmer of light,
And the solitude sleeps,—
Then I lie in my bunk wide awake,
And my long thoughts stab me with longing,
Alone in my shack by the marshes of lone Margaree.

Far, oh so far in the forests of silence they lie,
The lake and the marshes of lone Margaree,
And no man comes my way.
Of spruce logs my cabin is builded securely;
With slender spruce saplings its bark roof is battened
 down surely;
In its rafters the mice are at play,
With rustlings furtive and shy,
In the still of the night.

Awake, wide-eyed, I watch my window-square,
Pallid and grey.
(O Memory, pierce me not! O Longing, stab me not!
O ache of longing memory, pass me by, and spare,
And let me sleep!)
Once and again the loon cries from the lake.
Though no breath stirs
The ghostly tamaracks and the brooding firs,
Something as light as air leans on my door.

Is it an owl's wing brushes at my latch?
Are they of foxes, those light feet that creep
Outside, light as fall'n leaves
On the forest floor?
From the still lake I hear
A feeding trout rise to some small night fly.
The splash, how sharply clear!
Almost I see the wide, slow ripple circling to the shore.

The spent winds are at rest.   But my heart, spent
        and faint, is unresting,
Long, long a stranger to peace   .   .   .
O so Dear, O so Far, O so Unforgotten-in-dream,
Somewhere in the world, somewhere beyond reach of
        my questing.
Beyond seas, beyond years,
You will hear my heart in your sleep, and you will
        stir restlessly;
You will stir at the touch of my hand on your hair;
You will wake with a start,
With my voice in your ears
And an old, old ache at your heart,
(In the still of the night)
And your pillow wet with tears.


## The Skater

My glad feet shod with the glittering steel
I was the god of the wingèd heel.

The hills in the far white sky were lost;
The world lay still in the wide white frost;

And the woods hung hushed in their long white dream
By the ghostly, glimmering, ice-blue stream.

Here was a pathway, smooth like glass,
Where I and the wandering wind might pass

To the far-off palaces, drifted deep,
Where Winter's retinue rests in sleep.

I followed the lure, I fled like a bird,
Till the startled hollows awoke and heard

A spinning whisper, a sibilant twang,
As the stroke of the steel on the tense ice rang;

And the wandering wind was left behind
As faster, faster I followed my mind;

Till the blood sang high in my eager brain,
And the joy of my flight was almost pain.

Then I stayed the rush of my eager speed
And silently went as a drifting seed,—

Slowly, furtively, till my eyes
Grew big with the awe of a dim surmise,

And the hair of my neck began to creep
At hearing the wilderness talk in sleep.

Shapes in the fir-gloom drifted near.
In the deep of my heart I heard my fear.

And I turned and fled, like a soul pursued,
From the white, inviolate solitude.

## The Chopping Bee

The morning star was bitter bright, the morning
    sky was grey;
And we hitched our teams and started for the woods
    at break of day.
    *Oh, the frost is on the forest, and the snow piles high!*

Along the white and winding road the sled-bells
    jangled keen
Between the buried fences, the billowy drifts between.
    *Oh, merry swing the axes, and the bright chips fly!*

So crisp sang the runners, and so swift the horses sped,
That the woods were all about us ere the sky grew red.
    *Oh, the frost is on the forest, and the snow piles high!*

The bark hung ragged on the birch, the lichen on the fir,
The lungwort fringed the maple, and grey moss the
    juniper.
    *Oh, merry swing the axes, and the bright chips fly!*

So still the air and chill the air the branches seemed
    asleep,
But we broke their ancient visions as the axe bit deep.
    *Oh, the frost is on the forest, and the snow piles high!*

With the shouts of the choppers and the barking of
    their blades
How rang the startled valleys and the rabbit-haunted
    glades!
    *Oh, merry swing the axes, and the bright chips fly!*

The hard wood and the soft wood, we felled them for
    our use;
And chiefly, for its scented gum, we loved the scaly
    spruce;
    *Oh, the frost is on the forest, and the snow piles high!*

And here and there, with solemn roar, some hoary
    tree came down,
And we heard the rolling of the years in the thunder
    of its crown.
    *Oh, merry swing the axes, and the bright chips fly!*

So, many a sled was loaded up above the stake-tops
    soon;
And many a load was at the farm before the horn of
    noon;
    *Oh, the frost is on the forest, and the snow piles high!*

And ere we saw the sundown all yellow through the trees,
The farmyard stood as thick with wood as a buckwheat
        patch with bees;
    *Oh, merry swing the axes, and the bright chips fly!*

And with the last-returning teams, and axes burnished
    bright,
We left the woods to slumber in the frosty shadowed
    night.
    *Oh, the frost is on the forest, and the snow piles high!*

And then the wide, warm kitchen, with beams across
    the ceiling,
Thick hung with red-skinned onions, and homely herbs
    of healing!
    *Oh, merry swing the axes, and the bright chips fly!*

The dishes on the dresser-shelves were shining blue
   and white,
And o'er the loaded table the lamps beamed bright.
   *Oh, the frost is on the forest, and the snow piles high!*

Then, how the ham and turkey and the apple-sauce
   did fly,
The heights of boiled potatoes and the flats of pumpkin-
   pie!
   *Oh, merry swing the axes, and the bright chips fly!*

With bread-and-cheese and doughnuts fit to feed a
   farm a year!
And we washed them down with tides of tea and
   oceans of spruce beer.
   *Oh, the frost is on the forest, and the snow piles high!*

At last the pipes were lighted and the chairs pushed
   back,
And Bill struck up a sea-song on a rather risky tack;
   *Oh, merry swing the axes, and the bright chips fly!*

And the girls all thought it funny—but they never
   knew 't was worse,
For we gagged him with a doughnut at the famous
   second verse.
   *Oh, the frost is on the forest, and the snow piles high!*

Then someone fetched a fiddle, and we shoved away
   the table,
And 't was jig and reel and polka just as long as we
   were able,
   *Oh, merry swing the axes, and the bright chips fly!*

Till at last the girls grew sleepy, and we got our coats
   to go.
We started off with racing-teams and moonlight on
   the snow;
   *Oh, the frost is on the forest, and the snow piles high!*

And soon again the winter world was voiceless as of old,
Alone with all the wheeling stars, and the great white
   cold.
   *Oh, the frost is on the forest, and the snow piles high!*

[ 47 ]

## In the Afternoon

Wind of the summer afternoon,
Hush, for my heart is out of tune!

Hush, for thou movest restlessly
The too light sleeper, memory!

Whate'er thou hast to tell me, yet
'T were something sweeter to forget,—

Sweeter than all thy breath of balm
An hour of unremembering calm.

Blowing over the roofs, and down
The bright streets of this inland town,

These busy crowds, these rocking trees—
What strange note hast thou caught from these?

A note of waves and rushing tides,
Where past the dykes the red flood glides,

To brim the shining channels far
Up the green plains of Tantramar.

Once more I sniff the salt, I stand
On the long dykes of Westmoreland;

I watch the narrowing flats, the strip
Of red clay at the water's lip;

Far off the net-reels, brown and high,
And boat-masts slim against the sky;

Along the ridges of the dykes
Wind-beaten scant sea-grass, and spikes

Of last year's mullein; down the slopes
To landward, in the sun, thick ropes

Of blue vetch and convolvulus
And matted roses glorious.

The liberal blooms o'erbrim my hands;
I walk the level, wide marsh-lands;

Waist-deep in dusty-blossomed grass
I watch the swooping breezes pass

In sudden, long, pale lines, that flee
Up the deep breast of this green sea.

I listen to the bird that stirs
The purple tops, and grasshoppers

Whose summer din, before my feet
Subsiding, wakes on my retreat.

Again the droning bees hum by;
Still-winged, the grey hawk wheels on high;

I drink again the wild perfumes,
And roll, and crush the grassy blooms

Blown back to olden days, I fain
Would quaff the olden joys again;

But all the olden sweetness not
The old unmindful peace hath brought.

Wind of this summer afternoon,
Thou hast recalled my childhood's June.

My heart—still is it satisfied
By all the golden summer-tide?

Hast thou one eager yearning filled,
Or any restless throbbing stilled,

Or hast thou any power to bear
Even a little of my care?—

Ever so little of this weight
Of weariness canst thou abate?

Ah, poor thy gift indeed, unless
Thou bring the old child-heartedness,—

And such a gift to bring is given,
Alas, to no wind under heaven!

Wind of the summer afternoon,
Be still; my heart is not in tune.

Sweet is thy voice; but yet, but yet—
Of all 't were sweetest to forget!

# Tantramar Revisited

Summers and summers have come, and gone with the
    flight of the swallow;
Sunshine and thunder have been, storm, and winter,
    and frost;
Many and many a sorrow has all but died from remem-
    brance,
Many a dream of joy fall'n in the shadow of pain.
Hands of chance and change have marred, or moulded,
    or broken,
Busy with spirit or flesh, all I most have adored;
Even the bosom of Earth is strewn with heavier
    shadows,—
Only in these green hills, aslant to the sea, no change!
Here where the road that has climbed from the inland
    valleys and woodlands,
Dips from the hill-tops down, straight to the base of
    the hills,—
Here, from my vantage-ground, I can see the scattering
    houses,
Stained with time, set warm in orchards, meadows,
    and wheat,
Dotting the broad bright slopes outspread to south-
    ward and eastward,
Wind-swept all day long, blown by the south-east wind.

Skirting the sunbright uplands stretches a riband of
    meadow,
Shorn of the labouring grass, bulwarked well from the
    sea,
Fenced on its seaward border with long clay dykes
    from the turbid
Surge and flow of the tides vexing the Westmoreland
    shores.
Yonder, toward the left, lie broad the Westmoreland
    marshes,—
Miles on miles they extend, level, and grassy, and dim,
Clear from the long red sweep of flats to the sky in the
    distance,
Save for the outlying heights, green-rampired Cumber-
    land Point;
Miles on miles outrolled, and the river-channels divide
    them,—
Miles on miles of green, barred by the hurtling gusts.

Miles on miles beyond the tawny bay is Minudie.
There are the low blue hills; villages gleam at their feet.
Nearer a white sail shines across the water, and nearer
Still are the slim, grey masts of fishing boats dry on
   the flats.
Ah, how well I remember those wide red flats, above
   tide-mark
Pale with scurf of the salt, seamed and baked in the
   sun!
Well I remember the piles of blocks and ropes, and the
   net-reels
Wound with the beaded nets, dripping and dark from
   the sea!
Now at this season the nets are unwound; they hang
   from the rafters
Over the fresh-stowed hay in upland barns, and the
   wind
Blows all day through the chinks, with the streaks of
   sunlight, and sways them
Softly at will; or they lie heaped in the gloom of a loft.

Now at this season the reels are empty and idle; I see
   them
Over the lines of the dykes, over the gossiping grass.
Now at this season they swing in the long strong wind,
   thro' the lonesome
Golden afternoon, shunned by the foraging gulls.
Near about sunset the crane will journey homeward
   above them;
Round them, under the moon, all the calm night long,
Winnowing soft grey wings of marsh-owls wander
   and wander,
Now to the broad, lit marsh, now to the dusk of the
   dike.
Soon, thro' their dew-wet frames, in the live keen
   freshness of morning,
Out of the teeth of the dawn blows back the awakening
   wind.
Then, as the blue day mounts, and the low-shot shafts
   of the sunlight
Glance from the tide to the shore, gossamers jewelled
   with dew
Sparkle and wave, where late sea-spoiling fathoms of
   drift-net
Myriad-meshed, uploomed sombrely over the land.

Well I remember it all.   The salt, raw scent of the
    margin;
While, with men at the windlass, groaned each reel,
    and the net,
Surging in ponderous lengths, uprose and coiled in its
    station;
Then each man to his home,—well I remember it all!

Yet, as I sit and watch, this present peace of the
    landscape,—
Stranded boats, these reels empty and idle, the hush,
One grey hawk slow-wheeling above yon cluster of
    haystacks,—
More than the old-time stir this stillness welcomes me
    home.
Ah, the old-time stir, how once it stung me with
    rapture,—
Old-time sweetness, the winds freighted with honey
    and salt!
Yet will I stay my steps and not go down to the
    marshland,—
Muse and recall far off, rather remember than see,—
Lest on too close sight I miss the darling illusion,
Spy at their task even here the hands of chance and
    change.


## On the Creek

Dear Heart, the noisy strife
    And bitter carpings cease.
Here is the lap of life,
    Here are the lips of peace.

Afar from stir of streets,
    The city's dust and din,
What healing silence meets
    And greets us gliding in!

Our light birch silent floats;
    Soundless the paddle dips.
Yon sunbeam thick with motes
    Athro' the leafage slips,

[ 52 ]

To light the iris wings
  Of dragon-flies alit
On lily-leaves, and things
  Of gauze that float and flit.

Above the water's brink
  Hush'd winds make summer riot;
Our thirsty spirits drink
  Deep, deep, the summer quiet.

We slip the world's grey husk,
  Emerge, and spread new plumes;
In sunbeam-fretted dusk,
  Thro' populous golden glooms,

Like thistledown we slide,
  Two disembodied dreams,—
With spirits alert, wide-eyed,
  Explore the perfume-streams.

For scents of various grass
  Stream down the veering breeze;
Warm puffs of honey pass
  From flowering linden-trees;

And fragrant gusts of gum,
  Breath of the balm-tree buds,
With fern-brake odours, come
  From intricate solitudes.

The elm-tops are astir
  With flirt of idle wings.
Hark to the grackles' *chirr*
  Whene'er an elm-bough swings!

From off yon ash-limb sere
  Out-thrust amid green branches,
Keen like an azure spear
  A kingfisher down launches.

Far up the creek his calls
  And lessening laugh retreat.
Again the silence falls,
  And soft the green hours fleet.

[ 53 ]

They fleet with drowsy hum
　　Of insects on the wing.
We sigh—the end must come!
　　We taste our pleasure's sting.

No more, then, need we try
　　The rapture to regain.
We feel our day slip by,
　　And cling to it in vain.

But, Dear, keep thou in mind
　　These moments swift and sweet!
Their memory thou shalt find
　　Illume the common street;

And thro' the dust and din,
　　Smiling, thy heart shall hear
Quiet waters lapsing thin,
　　And locusts shrilling clear.

## The Deserted Wharf

The long tides sweep
　　Around its sleep,
The long red tides of Tantramar.
　　Around its dream
　　They hiss and stream,
Sad for the ships that have sailed afar.

*How many lips*
　　*Have lost their bloom,*
*How many ships*
　　*Gone down to gloom,*
*Since keel and sail*
　　*Have fled out from me*
*Over the thunder and strain of the sea!*

Its kale-dark sides
　　Throb in the tides;
The long winds over it spin and hum;
　　Its timbers ache
　　For memory's sake,
And the throngs that never again will come.

*How many lips*
  *Have lost their bloom,*
*How many ships*
  *Gone down to gloom,*
*Since keel and sail*
  *Have fled out from me*
*Over the thunder and strain of the sea!*

## The Trout Brook

The airs that blew from the brink of day
Were fresh and wet with the breath of May.
I heard the babble of brown brooks falling
And golden-wings in the woodside calling.

Big drops hung from the sparkling eaves;
And through the screen of the thin young leaves
A glint of ripples, a whirl of foam,
Lured and beckoned me out from home.

My feet grew eager, my eyes grew wide,
And I was off by the brown brook's side.
Down in the swamp-bottom, cool and dim,
I cut me an alder sapling slim.

With nimble fingers I tied my line,
Clear as a sunbeam, strong and fine.
My fly was a tiny glittering thing,
With tinsel body and partridge wing.

With noiseless steps I threaded the wood,
Glad of the sun-pierced solitude.
Chattered the kingfisher, fierce and shy,
  As like a shadow I drifted by.

Lurked in their watery lairs the trout,
But, silver and scarlet, I lured them out.
Wary were they, but warier still
My cunning wrist and my cast of skill.

I whipped the red pools under the beeches;
I whipped the yellow and dancing reaches.
The purple eddy, smooth like oil,
And the tail of the rapid yielded spoil.

[ 55 ]

So all day long, till the day was done,
I followed the stream, I followed the sun.
Then homeward over the ridge I went,
The wandering heart of me well content.

## In the Barn-Yard's Southerly Corner

When the frost is white on the fodder-stack,
The haws in the thorn-bush withered and black,
When the near fields flash in a diamond mail
And the far hills glimmer opaline pale,
Oh, merrily shines the morning sun
   In the barn-yard's southerly corner.

When the ruts in the cart-road ring like steel
And the birds to the kitchen door come for their meal,
And the snow at the gate is lightly drifted
And over the wood-pile thinly sifted,
Oh, merrily shines the morning sun
   In the barn-yard's southerly corner.

When the brimming bucket steams at the well,
And the axe on the beech-knot sings like a bell,
When the pond is loud with the skaters' calls,
And the horses stamp in the littered stalls,
Oh, merrily shines the morning sun
   In the barn-yard's southerly corner.

When the hay lies loose on the wide barn-floor,
And a sharp smell puffs from the stable door,
When the pitchfork handle stings in the hand
And the stanchioned cows for the milking stand,
Oh, merrily shines the morning sun
   In the barn-yard's southerly corner.

And the steers, let out for a drink and a run
Seek the warm corner one by one,
And the huddling sheep, in their dusty white,
Nose at the straw in the pleasant light,
When merrily shines the morning sun
   In the barn-yard's southerly corner.

# The Farmer's Winter Morning

The wide, white world is bitter still,
   (Oh, the snow lies deep in the barn-yard.)
And the dawn bites hard on the naked hill;
And the kitchen smoke from the chimney curls
Unblown, and hangs with a hue of pearls.
   (Oh, the snow lies deep in the barn-yard.)

The polished well-iron burns like a brand.
   (Oh, the frost is white on the latch.)
The horses neigh for their master's hand;
In the dusky stable they paw the floor
As his steps come crunching up to the door.
   (Oh, the frost is white on the latch.)

In the high, dim barn the smell of the hay
   (Oh, the snow lies deep in the barn-yard.)
Breathes him the breath of a summer's day.
The cows in their stanchions heavily rise
And watch him with slow, expectant eyes
   (Oh, the snow lies deep in the barn-yard.)

Into the mangers, into the stalls,
   (Oh, the frost is white on the latch.)
The fodder, cheerily rustling, falls.
And the sound of the feeding fills the air
As the sun looks in at the window-square.
   (Oh, the frost is white on the latch.)

With a rhythmic din in the echoing tins
   (Oh, the snow lies deep in the barn-yard.)
The noise of the milking soon begins.
With deepening murmur up to the brims
The foamy whiteness gathers and swims.
   (Oh, the snow lies deep in the barn-yard.)

When the ice is chopped at the great trough's brink,
   (Oh, the frost is white on the latch.)
The cattle come lazily out to drink;
And the fowls come out on the sun-lit straw,—
For the sun's got high, and the south eaves thaw,
   (And the frost is gone from the latch.)

[ 57 ]

# Marjory

Spring, summer, autumn, winter,
  Over the wild world rolls the year.
Comes June to the rose-red tamarack buds,
  But Marjory comes not here.

The pastures miss her; the house without her
  Grows forgotten, and grey and old;
The wind, and the lonely light of the sun
  Are heavy with tears untold.

Spring, summer, autumn, winter,
  Morning, evening, over and o'er!
The swallow returns to the nested rafter,
  But Marjory comes no more.

The grey barn-doors in the long wind rattle
  Hour by hour of the long white day.
The horses fret by the well-filled manger
  Since Marjory went away.

The sheep she fed at the bars await her.
  The milch cows low for her down the lane.
They long for her light, light hand at the milking,—
  They long for her hand in vain.

Spring, summer, autumn, winter,
  Morning and evening, over and o'er!
The bees come back with the willow catkins,
  But Marjory comes no more.

The voice of the far-off city called to her.
  Was it long years or an hour ago?
She went away, with dear eyes weeping,
  To a world she did not know.

The berried pastures they could not keep her,
  The brook, nor the buttercup-golden hill,
Nor even the long, long love familiar,—
  The strange voice called her still.

She would not stay for the old home garden;—
  The scarlet poppy, the mignonette,
The fox-glove bell, and the kind-eyed pansy,
  Their hearts will not forget.

Oh, that her feet had not forgotten
   The woodland country, the homeward way!
Oh, to look out of the sad, bright window
   And see her come back, some day!

Spring, summer, autumn, winter,
   Over the wild world rolls the year.
Comes joy to the bird on the nested rafter;
   But Marjory comes not here.


## The Heal-All

Dear blossom of the wayside kin,
   Whose homely, wholesome name
Tells of a potency within
   To win thee country fame!

The sterile hillocks are thy home,
   Beside the windy path;
The sky, a pale and lonely dome,
   Is all thy vision hath.

Thy unobtrusive purple face
   Amid the meagre grass
Greets me with long-remembered grace,
   And cheers me as I pass.

And I, outworn by petty care,
   And vexed with trivial wrong,
I heed thy brave and joyous air
   Until my heart grows strong.

A lesson from the Power I crave
   That moves in me and thee,
That makes thee modest, calm, and brave,—
   Me restless as the sea.

Thy simple wisdom I would gain,—
   To heal the hurt Life brings,
With kindly cheer, and faith in pain,
   And joy of common things.

[ 59 ]

## Apple Song

O the sun has kissed the apples,
    Kissed the apples;
And the apples, hanging mellow,
    Red and yellow,
All down the orchard seen
Make a glory in the green.

The sun has kissed the apples,
    Kissed the apples;
And the hollow barrels wait
    By the gate.
The cider-presses drip
With nectar for the lip.

The sun has kissed the apples,
    Kissed the apples;
And the yellow miles of grain
    Forget the rain.
The happy gardens yet
The winter's blight forget.

The sun has kissed the apples,
    Kissed the apples;
O'er the marsh the cattle spread,
    White and red.
The sky is all as blue
As a gentian in the dew.

The sun has kissed the apples,
    Kissed the apples;
And the maples are ablaze
    Through the haze.
The crickets in their mirth
Fife the fruiting song of earth.

The sun has kissed the apples,
    Kissed the apples;
Now with flocking call and stir
    Birds confer,
As if their hearts were crost
By a fear of coming frost.

[ 60 ]

O the sun has kissed the apples,
  Kissed the apples;
And the harvest air is sweet
  On the wheat.
Delight is not for long,—
Give us laughter, give us song!


## The Silver Thaw

There came a day of showers
  Upon the shrinking snow.
The south wind sighed of flowers,
  The softening skies hung low.
Midwinter for a space
Foreshadowing April's face,
The white world caught the fancy,
  And would not let it go.

In reawakened courses
  The brooks rejoiced the land.
We dreamed the Spring's shy forces
  Were gathering close at hand.
The dripping buds were stirred,
As if the sap had heard
The long-desired persuasion
  Of April's soft command.

But antic Time had cheated
  With hope's elusive gleam.
The phantom Spring, defeated,
  Fled down the ways of dream.
And in the night the reign
Of Winter came again,
With frost upon the forest
  And stillness on the stream.

When morn in rose and crocus
  Came up the bitter sky,
Celestial beams awoke us
  To wondering ecstasy.
The wizard Winter's spell
Had wrought so passing well,
That earth was bathed in glory,
  As if God's smile were nigh.

[ 61 ]

The silvered saplings, bending,
  Flashed in a rain of gems.
The statelier trees, attending,
  Blazed in their diadems.
White fire and amethyst
All common things had kissed,
And chrysolites and sapphires
  Adorned the bramble-stems.

In crystalline confusion
  All beauty came to birth.
It was a kind illusion
  To comfort waiting earth—
To bid the buds forget
The Spring so distant yet,
And hearts no more remember
  The iron season's dearth.


## A Song for April

List! list!  The buds confer.
This noonday they've had news of her;
The south bank has had views of her;
The thorn shall exact his dues of her;
    The willows adream
    By the freshet stream
Shall ask what boon they choose of her.

Up! up!  The world's astir;
The would-be green has word of her;
Root and germ have heard of her,
    Coming to break
    Their sleep and wake
Their hearts with every bird of her.

See! see!  How swift concur
Sun, wind, and rain at the name of her,
A-wondering what became of her;
The fields flower at the flame of her;
    The glad air sings
    With dancing wings
And the silvery shrill acclaim of her.

[ 62 ]

# Birch and Paddle

### To Bliss Carman

Friend, those delights of ours
Under the sun and showers,—

Athrough the noonday blue
Sliding our light canoe,

Or floating, hushed, at eve,
Where the dim pine-tops grieve!

What tonic days were they
Where shy streams dart and play,—

Where rivers brown and strong
As caribou bound along,

Break into angry parle
Where wildcat rapids snarl,

Subside, and like a snake
Wind to the quiet lake!

We've paddled furtively,
Where giant boughs hide the sky,—

Have stolen, and held our breath,
Thro' coverts still as death,—

Have left with wing unstirred
The brooding phœbe-bird,

And hardly caused a care
In the water-spider's lair.

For love of his clear pipe
We've flushed the zigzag snipe,—

Have chased in wilful mood
The wood-duck's flapping brood,—

Have spied the antlered moose
Cropping the young green spruce,

[ 63 ]

And watched him till betrayed
By the kingfisher's sharp tirade.

Quitting the bodeful shades
We've run thro' sunnier glades,

And dropping craft and heed
Have bid our paddles speed.

Where the mad rapids chafe
We've shouted, steering safe,—

With sinew tense, nerve keen,
Shot thro' the roar, and seen,

With spirit wild as theirs,
The white waves leap like hares.

And then, with souls grown clear
In that sweet atmosphere,

With influences serene
Our blood and brain washed clean,

We've idled down the breast
Of broadening tides at rest,

And marked the winds, the birds,
The bees, the far-off herds,

Into a drowsy tune
Transmute the afternoon.

So, Friend, with ears and eyes
Which shy divinities

Have opened with their kiss,
We need no balm but this,—

A little space for dreams
On care-unsullied streams,—

'Mid task and toil, a space
To dream on Nature's face!

## Up and Away in the Morning

Tide's at full; the waves break white.
    (Oh, up and away in the morning!)
Blue is the blown grass, red is the height;
Washed with the sun the sail shines white.
    (Oh, up and away in the morning!)

Wide is the world in the laughing sun.
    (Oh, up and away in the morning!)
Work 's to be done and wealth 's to be won
Ere a man turn home with the homing sun.
    (Oh, up and away in the morning!)

Long is the heart's hope, long as the day.
    (Oh, up and away in the morning!)
Heart has its will and hand has its way
Till the world rolls over and ends the day.
    (Oh, up and away in the morning!)

It 's home that we toil for all day long.
    (Oh, up and away in the morning!)
Hand on the line and heart in the song,
The labour of love will not seem long.
    (Oh, up and away in the morning!)


## Home, Home in the Evening

When the crows fly in from sea
    (Oh, home, home in the evening!)
My love in his boat comes back to me,
Over the tumbling leagues of sea.
    (Oh, home, home in the evening!)

And when the sun drops over the hill
    (Oh, home, home in the evening!)
My happy eyes they take their fill
Of watching my love as he climbs the hill.
    (Oh, home, home in the evening!)

[ 65 ]

And when the dew falls over the land
  (Oh, home, home in the evening!)
I hold in my hand his dearest hand,
The happiest woman in all the land.
  (Oh, home, home in the evening!)

    \*      \*      \*      \*      \*

All day she sang by the cottage door.
  (Oh, home, home in the evening!)
At sundown came his boat to the shore—
But he to the hearthside comes no more
  Home, home in the evening.

IV.  Poems Philosophical and
Mystical

# Child of the Infinite

Sun, and Moon, and Wind, and Flame,
Dust, and Dew, and Day and Night,—
Ye endure.  Shall I endure not,
Though so fleeting in your sight?
Ye return.  Shall I return not,
Flesh, or in the flesh's despite?
Ye are mighty.  But I hold you
Compassed in a vaster might.

*Sun.*   Sun, before your flaming circuit
Smote upon the uncumbered dark,
I, within the Thought Eternal
Palpitant, a quenchless spark,
Watched while God awoke and set you
For a measure and a mark.

*Moon.*   Dove of Heaven, ere you brooded
Whitely o'er the shoreless waste
And upon the driven waters
Your austere enchantment placed,
I was power in God's conception,
Without rest and without haste.

*Wind.*   Breath of Time, before your whisper
Wandered o'er the naked world,
Ere your wrath from pole to tropic
Running Alps of ocean hurled,
I, the germ of storm in stillness,
At the heart of God lay furled.

*Flame.*   Journeying Spirit, ere your tongues
Taught the perished to aspire,
Charged the clod, and called the mortal
Through the reinitiant fire,
I was of the fiery impulse
Urging the Divine Desire.

*Dust.*   Seed of Earth, when down the void
You were scattered from His hand,
When the spinning clot contracted,
Globed and greened at His command,
I, behind the sifting fingers,
Saw the scheme of beauty planned.

[ 69 ]

*Dew.* Phantom of the Many Waters,
When no more you fleet and fall,
When no more your round you follow,
Infinite, ephemeral,
At the feet of the Unsleeping
I shall toss you like a ball.

*Day and* Rolling Masks of Life and Death,
*Night.* When no more your ancient place
Knows you, when your light and darkness
Swing no longer over space,
My remembrance shall restore you
To the favour of His face.

## Origins

Out of the dreams that heap
The hollow hand of sleep,—
Out of the dark sublime,
The echoing deeps of time,—
From the averted Face
Beyond the bournes of space,
Into the sudden sun
We journey, one by one.
Out of the hidden shade
Wherein desire is made,—
Out of the pregnant stir
Where death and life confer,—
The dark and mystic heat
Where soul and matter meet,—
The enigmatic Will,—
We start, and then are still.

Inexorably decreed
By the ancestral deed,
The puppets of our sires,
We work out blind desires,
And for our sons ordain
The blessing or the bane.
In ignorance we stand
With fate on either hand,
And question stars and earth
Of life, and death, and birth.

[ 70 ]

With wonder in our eyes
We scan the kindred skies,
While through the common grass
Our atoms mix and pass.
We feel the sap go free
When spring comes to the tree;
And in our blood is stirred
What warms the brooding bird.
The vital fire we breathe
That bud and blade bequeath,
And strength of native clay
In our full veins hath sway.

But in the urge intense
And fellowship of sense,
Suddenly comes a word
In other ages heard.
On a great wind our souls
Are borne to unknown goals,
And past the bournes of space
To the unaverted Face.


## Autochthon

### I

I am the spirit astir
    To swell the grain
When fruitful suns confer
    With labouring rain;
I am the life that thrills
    In branch and bloom;
I am the patience of abiding hills,
    The promise masked in doom.

### II

When the sombre lands are wrung
    And storms are out,
And giant woods give tongue,
    I am the shout;
And when the earth would sleep,
    Wrapped in her snows,
I am the infinite gleam of eyes that keep
    The post of her repose.

III

I am the hush of calm,
   I am the speed,
The flood-tide's triumphing psalm,
   The marsh-pool's heed;
I work in the rocking roar
   Where cataracts fall;
I flash in the prismy fire that dances o'er
   The dew's ephemeral ball.

IV

I am the voice of wind
   And wave and tree,
Of stern desires and blind,
   Of strength to be;
I am the cry by night
   At point of dawn,
The summoning bugle from the unseen height,
   In cloud and doubt withdrawn.

V

I am the strife that shapes
   The stature of man,
The pang no hero escapes,
   The blessing, the ban;
I am the hammer that moulds
   The iron of our race,
The omen of God in our blood that a people beholds,
   The foreknowledge veiled in our face.

### The Unsleeping

I soothe to unimagined sleep
The sunless bases of the deep.
And then I stir the aching tide
That gropes in its reluctant side.

I heave aloft the smoking hill;
To silent peace its throes I still.
But ever at its heart of fire
I lurk, an unassuaged desire.

[ 72 ]

I wrap me in the sightless germ
An instant or an endless term;
And still its atoms are my care,
Dispersed in ashes or in air.

I hush the comets one by one
To sleep for ages in the sun;
The sun resumes before my face
His circuit of the shores of space.

The mount, the star, the germ, the deep,
They all shall wake, they all shall sleep.
Time, like a flurry of wild rain,
Shall drift across the darkened pane.

Space, in the dim predestined hour,
Shall crumble like a ruined tower.
I only, with unfaltering eye,
Shall watch the dreams of God go by.


## Recessional

Now along the solemn heights
Fade the Autumn's altar-lights;
   Down the great earth's glimmering chancel
Glide the days and nights.

Little kindred of the grass,
Like a shadow in a glass
   Falls the dark and falls the stillness;
We must rise and pass.

We must rise and follow, wending
Where the nights and days have ending,—
   Pass in order pale and slow
Unto sleep extending.

Little brothers of the clod,
Soul of fire and seed of sod,
   We must fare into the silence
At the knees of God.

[ 73 ]

Little comrades of the sky
Wing to wing we wander by,
   Going, going, going, going,
Softly as a sigh.

Hark, the moving shapes confer,
Globe of dew and gossamer,
   Fading and ephemeral spirits
In the dusk astir.

Moth and blossom, blade and bee,
Worlds must go as well as we,
   In the long procession joining
Mount, and star, and sea.

Toward the shadowy brink we climb
Where the round year rolls sublime,
   Rolls, and drops, and falls forever
In the vast of time.

## Afoot

Comes the lure of green things growing,
Comes the call of waters flowing,—
   And the wayfarer Desire
Moves and wakes and would be going.

Hark the migrant hosts of June
Marching nearer noon by noon!
   Hark the gossip of the grasses
Bivouacked beneath the moon!

Hark the leaves their mirth averring;
Hark the buds to blossom stirring;
   Hark the hushed, exultant haste
Of the wind and world conferring!

Hark the sharp, insistent cry
Where the hawk patrols the sky!
   Hark the flapping, as of banners,
Where the heron triumphs by!

Empire in the coasts of bloom
Humming cohorts now resume,—
   And desire is forth to follow
Many a vagabond perfume.

Long the quest and far the ending
Where my wayfarer is wending,—
    When Desire is once afoot,
Doom behind and Dream attending!

Shuttle-cock of indecision,
Sport of chance's blind derision,
    Yet he may not fail nor tire
Till his eyes shall win the Vision

In his ears the phantom chime
Of incommunicable rhyme,
    He shall chase the fleeting camp-fires
Of the Bedouins of Time.

Farer by uncharted ways,
Dumb as Death to plaint or praise,
    Unreturning he shall journey,
Fellow to the nights and days;

Till upon the outer bar
Stilled the moaning currents are,
    Till the flame achieves the zenith,
Till the moth attains the star,

Till, through laughter and through tears,
Fair the final peace appears,
    And about the watered pastures
Sink to sleep the nomad years!


## The Falling Leaves

Lightly He blows, and at His breath they fall,
    The perishing kindreds of the leaves; they drift,
Spent flames of scarlet, gold aërial,
    Across the hollow year, noiseless and swift.
Lightly He blows, and countless as the falling
    Of snow by night upon a solemn sea,
The ages circle down beyond recalling
    To strew the hollows of Eternity.
He sees them drifting through the spaces dim.
And leaves and ages are as one to Him

[ 75 ]

## The Great and the Little Weavers

The great and the little weavers,
They neither rest nor sleep.
They work in the height and the glory,
They toil in the dark and the deep.

The rainbow melts with the shower,
The white-thorn falls in the gust,
The cloud-rose dies into shadow,
The earth-rose dies into dust.

But they have not faded forever,
They have not flowered in vain,
For the great and the little weavers
Are weaving under the rain.

Recede the drums of the thunder
When the Titan chorus tires,
And the bird-song piercing the sunset
Faints with the sunset fires,

But the trump of the storm shall fail not,
Nor the flute-cry fail of the thrush,
For the great and the little weavers
Are weaving under the hush.

The comet flares into darkness,
The flame dissolves into death,
The power of the star and the dew
They grow and are gone like a breath,

But ere the old wonder is done
Is the new-old wonder begun,
For the great and the little weavers
Are weaving under the sun.

The domes of an empire crumble,
A child's hope dies in tears;
Time rolls them away forgotten
In the silt of the flooding years;

The creed for which men died smiling
Decays to a beldame's curse;
The love that made lips immortal
Drags by in a tattered hearse.

But not till the search of the moon
Sees the last white face uplift,
And over the bones of the kindreds
The bare sands dredge and drift,

Shall Love forget to return
And lift the unused latch,
(In his eyes the look of the traveller,
On his lips the foreign catch),

Nor the mad song leave men cold,
Nor the high dream summon in vain,—
For the great and the little weavers
Are weaving in heart and brain.

## Kinship

Back to the bewildering vision
    And the borderland of birth;
Back into the looming wonder,
    The companionship of earth;

Back unto the simple kindred—
    Childlike fingers, childlike eyes,
Working, waiting, comprehending,
    Now in patience, now surprise;

Back unto the faithful healing
    And the candour of the sod—
Scent of mould and moisture stirring
    At the secret touch of God;

Back into the ancient stillness
    Where the wise enchanter weaves,
To the twine of questing tree-root,
    The expectancy of leaves;

Back to hear the hushed consulting
    Over bud and blade and germ,
As the Mother's mood apportions
    Each its pattern, each its term;

Back into the grave beginnings
    Where all wonder-tales are true,
Strong enchantments, strange successions,
    Mysteries of old and new;

Back to knowledge and renewal,
  Faith to fashion and reveal,
Take me, Mother,—in compassion
  All thy hurt ones fain to heal.

Back to wisdom take me, Mother;
  Comfort me with kindred hands;
Tell me tales the world 's forgetting,
  Till my spirit understands.

Tell me how some sightless impulse,
  Working out a hidden plan,
God for kin and clay for fellow,
  Wakes to find itself a man.

Tell me how the life of mortal,
  Wavering from breath to breath,
Like a web of scarlet pattern
  Hurtles from the loom of death.

How the caged bright bird, desire,
  Which the hands of God deliver,
Beats aloft to drop unheeded
  At the confines of forever;

Faints unheeded for a season,
  Then outwings the farthest star,
To the wisdom and the stillness
  Where thy consummations are.


### Ascription

O Thou who hast beneath Thy hand
The dark foundations of the land,—
The motion of whose ordered thought
An instant universe hath wrought,—

Who hast within Thine equal heed
The rolling sun, the ripening seed,
The azure of the speedwell's eye,
The vast solemnities of sky,—

[ 78 ]

Who hear'st no less the feeble note
Of one small bird's awakening throat,
Than that unnamed, tremendous chord
Arcturus sounds before his Lord,—

More sweet to Thee than all acclaim
Of storm and ocean, stars and flame,
In favour more before Thy face
Than pageantry of time and space,

The worship and the service be
Of him Thou madest most like Thee,—
Who in his nostrils hath Thy breath,
Whose spirit is the lord of death!

## A Song of Growth

In the heart of a man
  Is a thought upfurled.
Reached its full span
  It shakes the world,
And to one high thought
Is a whole race wrought.

Not with vain noise
  The great work grows,
Nor with foolish voice,
  But in repose,—
Not in the rush
But in the hush.

From the cogent lash
  Of the cloud-herd wind
The low clouds dash,
  Blown headlong, blind;
But beyond, the great blue
Looks moveless through.

O'er the loud world sweep
  The scourge and the rod;
But in deep beyond deep
  Is the stillness of God,—
At the Fountains of Life
No cry, no strife.

[ 79 ]

## The Tower Beyond the Tops of Time

How long it was I did not know,
    That I had waited, watched, and feared.
It seemed a thousand years ago
    The last pale lights had disappeared.
I knew the place was a narrow room
Up, up beyond the reach of doom.

Then came a light more red than flame;—
    No sun-dawn, but the soul laid bare
Of earth and sky and sea became
    A presence burning everywhere;
And I was glad my narrow room
Was high above the reach of doom.

Windows there were in either wall,
    Deep cleft, and set with radiant glass,
Wherethrough I watched the mountains fall,
    The ages wither up and pass.
I knew their doom could never climb
My tower beyond the tops of Time.

A sea of faces then I saw,
    Of men who had been, men long dead.
Figured with dreams of joy and awe,
    The heavens unrolled in lambent red;
While far below the faces cried—
    "Give us the dream for which we died!"

Ever the woven shapes rolled by
    Above the faces hungering.
With quiet and incurious eye
    I noted many a wondrous thing,—
Seas of clear glass, and singing streams,
In that high pageantry of dreams;

Cities of sard and chrysoprase
    Where choired Hosannas never cease;
Valhallas of celestial frays,
    And lotus-pools of endless peace;
But still the faces gaped and cried—
    "Give us the dream for which we died!"

[ 80 ]

At length my quiet heart was stirred,
    Hearing them cry so long in vain.
But while I listened for a word
    That should translate them from their pain
I saw that here and there a face
Shone, and was lifted from its place,

And flashed into the moving dome
    An ecstasy of prismed fire.
And then said I, "A soul has come
    To the deep zenith of desire!"
But still I wondered if it knew
The dream for which it died was true.

I wondered—who shall say how long?
    (One heart-beat?—Thrice ten thousand years?)
Till suddenly there was no throng
    Of faces to arraign the spheres,—
No more white faces there to cry
To those great pageants of the sky.

Then quietly I grew aware
    Of one who came with eyes of bliss
And brow of calm and lips of prayer.
    Said I, "How wonderful is this!
Where are the faces once that cried—
'Give us the dream for which we died'?"

The answer fell as soft as sleep,—
    "I am of those who, having cried
So long in that tumultuous deep,
    Have won the dream for which we died."
And then said I, "Which dream was true?
For many were revealed to you!"

He answered, "To the soul made wise
    All true, all beautiful they seem.
But the white peace that fills our eyes
    Outdoes desire, outreaches dream.
For we are come unto the place
Where always we behold God's face!"

[ 81 ]

# The Vagrant of Time

I voyage north, I journey south,
   I taste the life of many lands,
With ready wonder in my eyes
   And strong adventure in my hands.

I join the young-eyed caravans
   That storm the portals of the West;
And sometimes in their throng I catch
   Hints of the secret of my quest.

The musks and attars of the East,
   Expecting marvels, I explore.
I chase them down the dim bazaar,
   I guess them through the close-shut door.

In the lone cabin, sheathed in snow,
   I bide a season, well content,
Till forth again I needs must fare,
   Called by an unknown continent.

I loiter down remembered shores
   Where restless tide-flows lift and surge,—
In my wild heart their restlessness
   And in my veins their tireless urge.

In old grey cities oft I dwell,
   Down storied rivers drift and dream.
Sometimes in palaces I lose,
   Sometimes in hovels catch, the gleam.

Great fortune in my wayfaring
   I stumble on, more oft than not,—
Grip comrade hands in hall or camp,
   Greet ardent lips in court or cot.

Down country lanes at noon I stray,
   Loaf in the homely wayside heat,
And with bright flies and droning bees
   Rifle the buckwheat of its sweet.

In solitudes of peak or plain,
   When vaulted space my sense unbars,
I pitch my tent, and camp the night
   Beyond the unfathomed gulfs of stars.

At times I thirst, at times I faint,
  Sink mired in swamp, stray blind in storm,
See high hopes shattered, faiths betrayed,—
  But stout heart keeps my courage warm.

And sometimes rock-ridged steeps I climb
  In chill black hours before the dawn.
With battered shins and bleeding feet
  And obstinate fists I blunder on.

And then, when sunrise floods my path,
  I pause to build my dreams anew.
But, take the gipsying all in all,
  I find a-many dreams come true.

So when, one night, I drop my pack
  Behind the Last Inn's shadowy door,
To take my rest in that lone room
  Where no guest ever lodged before,

In sleep too deep for dreams I'll lie,—
  Till One shall knock, and bid me rise
To quest new ventures, fare new roads,
  Essay new suns and vaster skies.


## The Hermit

Above the blindness of content,
  The ignorance of ease,
Inhabiting within his soul
  A shrine of memories,

Between the silences of sleep
  Attentively he hears
The endless crawling sob and strain,
  The spending of the years.

He sees the lapsing stream go by
  His unperturbèd face,
Out of a dark, into a dark,
  Across a lighted space.

He calls it Life, this lighted space
  Upon the moving flood.
He sees the water white with tears,
  He sees it red with blood.

[ 83 ]

And many specks upon the tide
  He sees and marks by name,—
Motes of a day, and fools of Fate,
  And challengers of fame;

With here a people, there a babe,
  A blossom, or a crown,—
They whirl a little, gleam, and pass,
  Or in the eddies drown.

He waits.   He waits one day to see
  The lapsing of the stream,
The eddying forms, the darknesses,
  Dissolve into a dream.

## When Mary the Mother Kissed the Child

When Mary the Mother kissed the Child
And night on the wintry hills grew mild,
And the strange star swung from the courts of air
To serve at a manger with kings in prayer,
Then did the day of the simple kin
And the unregarded folk begin.

When Mary the Mother forgot the pain,
In the stable of rock began love's reign.
When that new light on their grave eyes broke
The oxen were glad and forgot their yoke;
And the huddled sheep in the far hill fold
Stirred in their sleep and felt no cold.

When Mary the Mother gave of her breast
To the poor inn's latest and lowliest guest,—
The God born out of the woman's side,—
The Babe of Heaven by Earth denied,—
Then did the hurt ones cease to moan,
And the long-supplanted came to their own.

When Mary the Mother felt faint hands
Beat at her bosom with life's demands,
And naught to her were the kneeling kings,
The serving star and the half-seen wings,
Then was the little of earth made great,
And the man came back to the God's estate.

## In the Orchard

O apple leaves, so cool and green
    Against the summer sky,
You stir, although the wind is still
    And not a bird goes by.
      You start,
    And softly move apart
      In hushed expectancy.
Who is the gracious visitor
      Whose form I cannot see?

O apple leaves, the mystic light
    All down your dim arcade!
Why do your shadows tremble so,
    Half glad and half afraid?
      The air
    Is an unspoken prayer.
      Your eyes look all one way.
Who is the secret visitor
      Your tremors would betray?

## The Native

Rocks, I am one with you;
Sea, I am yours.
Your rages come and go,
Your strength endures.

Passion may burn and fade;
Pain surge and cease.
My still soul rests unchanged
Through storm and peace.

Fir-tree, beaten by wind,
Sombre, austere,
Your sap is in my veins
O kinsman dear.

Your fibres rude and true
My sinews feed—
Sprung of the same bleak earth,
The same rough seed.

[ 85 ]

The tempest harries us.
It raves and dies;
And wild limbs rest again
Under wide skies.

Grass, that the salt hath scourged,
Dauntless and grey,
Though the harsh season chide
Your scant array,

Year by year you return
To conquer fate.
The clean life nourishing you
Makes me, too, great.

O rocks, O fir-tree brave,
O grass and sea!
Your strength is mine, and you
Endure with me.

## On the Road

Ever just over the top of the next brown rise
I expect some wonderful thing to flatter my eyes.
"What's yonder?" I ask of the first wayfarer I meet.
"Nothing!" he answers, and looks at my travel-worn
   feet.

"Only more hills and more hills, like the many you've
   passed,
With rough country between, and a poor enough inn
   at the last."
But already I am a-move, for I see he is blind,
And I hate that old grumble I've listened to time
   out of mind.

I've tramped it too long not to know there is truth
   in it still,
That lure of the turn of the road, of the crest of the
   hill.
So I breast me the rise with full hope, well assured
   I shall see
Some new prospect of joy, some brave venture
   a-tiptoe for me.

For I have come far and confronted the calm and
the strife.
I have fared wide, and bit deep in the apple of life.
It is sweet at the rind, but oh, sweeter still at the
core;
And whatever be gained yet the reach of the morrow
is more.

At the crest of the hill I shall hail the new summits
to climb.
The demand of my vision shall beggar the largess
of time.
For I know that the higher I press, the wider I view,
The more's to be ventured and visioned, in worlds
that are new.

So when my feet, failing, shall stumble in ultimate
dark,
And faint eyes no more the high lift of the pathway
shall mark,
There under the dew I'll lie down with my dreams,
for I know
What bright hill-tops the morning will show me, all
red in the glow.

## To-day

As once by Hybna's emerald flow
    The goatboy saw in dream
The old gods to their hunting go,
    And heard their eagles scream,
    So I, by Nashwaak's amber stream,
See gods and heroes pass,
    While these drab days and deeds but seem
Like shadows in a glass.

But when a thousand years are done
    My eyes, unsealed, will know
Beauty and glory new begun
    As in the long ago;
    And then, astonished, I shall know
The splendour of To-day,
    When men outdare the old gods, and grow
In reach more vast than they.

## Hilltop Song

Here on the hill
At last the soul sees clear,
Desire being still,
The High Unseen appear.
The thin grass bends
One way, and hushed attends
Unknown and gracious ends.
Where the sheep's pasturing feet
Have cleft the sods
The mystic light lies sweet;
The very clods,
In purpling hues elate,
Thrill to their fate;
The high rock-hollows wait,
Expecting gods.

## Earth's Complines

Before the feet of the dew
There came a call I knew,
   Luring me into the garden
Where the tall white lilies grew.

I stood in the dusk between
The companies of green,
   O'er whose ethereal ranks
The lilies rose serene.

And the breathing air was stirred
By an unremembered word,
   Soft, incommunicable—
And wings not of a bird.

I heard the spent blooms sighing,
The expectant buds replying;
   I felt the life of the leaves,
Ephemeral, yet undying.

The spirits of earth were there,
Thronging the shadowed air,
   Serving among the lilies,
In an ecstasy of prayer.

Their speech I could not tell;
But the sap in each green cell,
    And the pure initiate petals,
They knew that language well.

I felt the soul of the trees—
Of the white, eternal seas—
    Of the flickering bats and night-moths
And my own soul kin to these.

And a spell came out of space
From the light of its starry place,
    And I saw in the deep of my heart
The image of God's face.


## O Earth, Sufficing All Our Needs

O earth, sufficing all our needs, O you
With room for body and for spirit too,
    How patient while your children vex their souls
Devising alien heavens beyond your blue!

Dear dwelling of the immortal and unseen,
How obstinate in my blindness have I been,
    Not comprehending what your tender calls,
Veiled promises and reassurance, mean.

Not far and cold the way that they have gone
Who through your sundering darkness have with-
        drawn;
    Almost within our hand-reach they remain
Who pass beyond the sequence of the dawn.

Not far and strange the Heaven, but very near,
Your children's hearts unknowingly hold dear.
    At times we almost catch the door swung wide.
An unforgotten voice almost we hear.

I am the heir of Heaven—and you are just.
You, you alone I know—and you I trust.
    I have sought God beyond His farthest star—
But here I find Him, in your quickening dust.

# The Unknown City

There lies a city inaccessible,
Where the dead dreamers dwell.


Abrupt and blue, with many a high ravine
And soaring bridge half seen,
With many an iris cloud that comes and goes
Over the ancient snows,
The imminent hills environ it, and hold
Its portals from of old,
That grief invade not, weariness, nor war.
Nor anguish evermore.


White-walled and jettied on the peacock tide,
With domes and towers enskied,
Its battlements and balconies one sheen
Of ever-living green,
It hears the happy dreamers turning home
Slow-oared across the foam.


Cool are its streets with waters musical
And fountains' shadowy fall.
With orange and anemone and rose
And every flower that blows
Of magic scent or unimagined dye,
Its gardens shine and sigh.
Its chambers, memoried with old romance
And faëry circumstance,—
From any window love may lean some time
For love that dares to climb.


This is that city babe and seer divined
With pure, believing mind.
This is the home of unachieved emprise.
Here, here the visioned eyes
Of them that dream past any power to do,
Wake to the dream come true.
Here the high failure, not the level fame,
Attests the spirit's aim.
Here is fulfilled each hope that soared and sought
Beyond the bournes of thought.

[ 90 ]

The obdurate marble yields; the canvas glows;
Perfect the column grows;
The chorded cadence art could ne'er attain
Crowns the imperfect strain;
And the great song that seemed to die unsung
Triumphs upon the tongue.


## Ballade of the Poet's Thought

A poet was vexed with the fume of the street,
  With tumult wearied, with din distraught;
And very few of the passing feet
  Would stay to listen the truths he taught.
  And he said,—"My labour is all for naught;
I will go, and at Nature's lips drink deep."
  For he knew not the wealth of the poet's thought,
Though sweet to win, was bitter to keep.

So he left the hurry, and dust, and heat
  For the free, green forest where man was not;
And found in the wilderness' deep retreat
  That favour with Nature which he sought.
  She spake with him, nor denied him aught,
In waking vision or visioned sleep,
  But little he guessed the wealth she brought,
Though sweet to win, was bitter to keep.

But now when his bosom, grown replete,
  Would lighten itself in song of what
It had gathered in silence, he could meet
  No answering thrill from his passion caught.
  Then grieving he fled from that quiet spot
To where men work, and are weary, and weep;
  For he said,—"The wealth for which I wrought
Is sweet to win, but bitter to keep."

ENVOI

Oh, poets, bewailing your hapless lot,
  That ye may not in Nature your whole hearts steep,
Know that the wealth of the poet's thought
  Is sweet to win, but bitter to keep.

[ 91 ]

## Wayfarer of Earth

Up, heart of mine,
Thou wayfarer of earth!
Of seed divine,
Be mindful of thy birth.
Though the flesh faint
Through long-endured constraint
Of nights and days,
Lift up thy praise
To life, that set thee in such strenuous ways,
And left thee not
To drowse and rot
In some thick-perfumed and luxurious plot.

Strong, strong is earth
With vigour for thy feet,
To make thy wayfaring
Tireless and fleet.
And good is earth,—
But earth not all thy good,
O thou with seed of suns
And star-fire in thy blood!

And though thou feel
The slow clog of the hours
Leaden upon thy heel,
Put forth thy powers.

Thine the deep sky,
The unpreëmpted blue,
The haste of storm,
The hush of dew.

Thine, thine the free
Exalt of star and tree,
The reinless run
Of wind and sun,
The vagrance of the sea.

## The Summons

Deeps of the wind-torn west,
  Flaming and desolate,
Upsprings my soul from his rest
  With your banners at the gate.

'Neath this o'ermastering sky
  How could the heart lie still,
  Or the sluggish will
Content in the old chains lie,
  When over the lonely hill
Your torn wild scarlets cry?

Up, Soul, and out
  Into the deeps alone,
To the long peal and the shout
  Of those trumpets blown and blown!

## The Aim

O Thou who lovest not alone
The swift success, the instant goal,
But hast a lenient eye to mark
The failures of the inconstant soul,

Consider not my little worth,—
The mean achievement, scamped in act,
The high resolve and low result,
The dream that durst not face the fact.

But count the reach of my desire.
Let this be something in Thy sight:—
I have not, in the slothful dark,
Forgot the Vision and the Height.

Neither my body nor my soul
To earth's low ease will yield consent.
I praise Thee for my will to strive.
I bless Thy goad of discontent.

## Hath Hope Kept Vigil

Frail lilies that beneath the dust so long
  Have lain in cerements of musk and slumber,
While over you hath fled the viewless throng
  Of hours and winds and voices out of number,

Pulseless and dead in that enswathing dark
  Hath hope kept vigil at your core of being?
Did the germ know what unextinguished spark
  Held these white blooms within its heart unseeing?

Once more into the dark when I go down,
  And deep and deaf the black clay seals my prison,
Will the numbed soul foreknow how light shall crown
  With strong young ecstasy its life new risen?


## Under the Pillars of the Sky

Under the pillars of the sky
I played at life, I knew not why.

The grave recurrence of the day
Was matter of my trivial play.

The solemn stars, the sacred night,
I took for toys of my delight,

Till now, with startled eyes, I see
The portents of Eternity.

# V. Sonnets of the Canadian Scene

## Prologue

Across the fog the moon lies fair.
  Transfused with ghostly amethyst,
O white Night, charm to wonderment
  The cattle in the mist!

Thy touch, O grave Mysteriarch,
  Makes dull, familiar things divine.
O grant of thy revealing gift
  Be some small portion mine!

Make thou my vision sane and clear,
  That I may see what beauty clings
In common forms, and find the soul
  Of unregarded things!


## The Flight of the Geese

I hear the low wind wash the softening snow,
  The low tide loiter down the shore.   The night,
  Full filled with April forecast, hath no light.
The salt wave on the sedge-flat pulses slow.
Through the hid furrows lisp in murmurous flow
  The thaw's shy ministers; and hark! The height
  Of heaven grows weird and loud with unseen flight
Of strong hosts prophesying as they go!

High through the drenched and hollow night their
      wings
  Beat northward hard on Winter's trail.   The sound
Of their confused and solemn voices, borne
Athwart the dark to their long Arctic morn,
  Comes with a sanction and an awe profound,
A boding of unknown, foreshadowed things.

[ 97 ]

# The Waking Earth

With shy bright clamour the live brooks sparkle and
    run.
Freed flocks confer about the farmstead ways.
The air's a wine of dreams and shining haze,
Beaded with bird-notes thin,—for Spring 's begun!
The sap flies upward.  Death is over and done.
    The glad earth wakes; the glad light breaks; the
    days
    Grow round, grow radiant.  Praise for the new life!
    Praise
For bliss of breath and blood beneath the sun!

What potent wizardry the wise earth wields,
To conjure with a perfume!  From bare fields
    The sense drinks in a breath of furrow and sod.
And lo, the bound of days and distance yields;
    And fetterless the soul is flown abroad,
    Lord of desire and beauty, like a god!


# The Sower

A brown, sad-coloured hillside, where the soil
    Fresh from the frequent harrow, deep and fine,
    Lies bare; no break in the remote sky-line,
Save where a flock of pigeons streams aloft,
Startled from feed in some low-lying croft,
    Or far-off spires with yellow of sunset shine;
    And here the Sower, unwittingly divine,
Exerts the silent forethought of his toil.

Alone he treads the glebe, his measured stride
    Dumb in the yielding soil; and though small joy
    Dwell in his heavy face, as spreads the blind
Pale grain from his dispensing palm aside,
    This plodding churl grows great in his employ;—
    God-like, he makes provision for mankind.

## When Milking Time Is Done

When milking-time is done, and over all
  This quiet Canadian inland forest home
  And wide rough pasture-lots the shadows come,
And dews, with peace and twilight voices, fall,
From moss-cooled watering-trough to foddered stall
  The tired plough-horses turn,—the barnyard loam
  Soft to their feet,—and in the sky's pale dome
Like resonant chords the swooping night-hawks call.

The frogs, cool-fluting ministers of dream,
  Make shrill the slow brook's borders; pasture bars
  Down clatter, and the cattle wander through,—
Vague shapes amid the thickets; gleam by gleam
  Above the wet grey wilds emerge the stars,
  And through the dusk the farmstead fades from view


## Frogs

Here in the red heart of the sunset lying,
  My rest an islet of brown weeds blown dry,
  I watch the wide bright heavens, hovering nigh,
My plain and pools in lucent splendour dyeing.
My view dreams over the rosy wastes, descrying
  The reed-tops fret the solitary sky;
  And all the air is tremulous to the cry
Of myriad frogs on mellow pipes replying.

For the unrest of passion here is peace,
  And eve's cool drench for midday soil and taint.
To tired ears how sweetly brings release
  This limpid babble from life's unstilled complaint;
  While under tired eyelids lapse and faint
The noon's derisive visions—fade and cease.

## The Cow Pasture

I see the harsh, wind-ridden, eastward hill,
  By the red cattle pastured, blanched with dew;
  The small, mossed hillocks where the clay gets
    through;
The grey webs woven on milkweed tops at will.
The sparse, pale grasses flicker, and are still.
  The empty flats yearn seaward.  All the view
  Is naked to the horizon's utmost blue;
And the bleak spaces stir me with strange thrill.

Not in perfection dwells the subtler power
  To pierce our mean content, but rather works
  Through incompletion, and the need that irks,—
Not in the flower, but effort toward the flower.
  When the want stirs, when the soul's cravings urge,
  The strong earth strengthens, and the clean heavens
    purge.


## The Herring Weir

Back to the green deeps of the outer bay
  The red and amber currents glide and cringe,
  Diminishing behind a luminous fringe
Of cream-white surf and wandering wraiths of spray.
Stealthily, in the old reluctant way,
  The red flats are uncovered, mile on mile,
  To glitter in the sun a golden while.
Far down the flats, a phantom sharply grey,

The herring weir emerges, quick with spoil.
  Slowly the tide forsakes it.   Then draws near,
  Descending from the farm-house on the height,
A cart, with gaping tubs.   The oxen toil
  Sombrely o'er the level to the weir,
  And drag a long black trail across the light.

## The Salt Flats

Here clove the keels of centuries ago
   Where now unvisited the flats lie bare.
   Here seethed the sweep of journeying waters, where
No more the tumbling floods of Fundy flow,
And only in the samphire pipes creep slow
   The salty currents of the sap.  The air
   Hums desolately with wings that seaward fare,
Over the lonely reaches beating low.

The wastes of hard and meagre weeds are thronged
With murmurs of a past that time has wronged;
   And ghosts of many an ancient memory
Dwell by the brackish pools and ditches blind,
In these low-lying pastures of the wind,
   These marshes pale and meadows by the sea.


## The Fir Woods

The wash of endless waves is in their tops,
   Endlessly swaying, and the long winds stream
   Athwart them from the far-off shores of dream.
Through the stirred branches filtering, faintly drops
Mystic dream-dust of isle, and palm, and cave,
   Coral and sapphire, realms of rose, that seem
   More radiant than ever earthly gleam
Revealed of fairy mead or haunted wave.

A cloud of gold, a cleft of blue profound,—
   These are my gates of wonder, surged about
   By tumult of tossed bough and rocking crest.
The vision lures.  The spirit spurns her bound,
   Spreads her unprisoned wing, and drifts from out
   This green and humming gloom that wraps my rest.

## The Pea-Fields

These are the fields of light, and laughing air,
  And yellow butterflies, and foraging bees,
  And whitish, wayward blossoms winged as these,
And pale green tangles like a seamaid's hair.
Pale, pale the blue, but pure beyond compare,
  And pale the sparkle of the far-off seas
  A-shimmer like these fluttering slopes of peas,
And pale the open landscape everywhere.

From fence to fence a perfumed breath exhales
  O'er the bright pallor of the well-loved fields,—
My fields of Tantramar in summer-time;
  And, scorning the poor feed their pasture yields,
Up from the bushy lots the cattle climb
  To gaze with longing through the grey, mossed rails.


## The Mowing

This is the voice of high midsummer's heat.
  The rasping vibrant clamour soars and shrills
  O'er all the meadowy range of shadeless hills,
As if a host of giant cicadae beat
The cymbals of their wings with tireless feet,
  Or brazen grasshoppers with triumphing note
  From the long swath proclaimed the fate that smote
The clover and timothy-tops and meadowsweet.

The crying knives glide on; the green swath lies.
  And all noon long the sun, with chemic ray,
  Seals up each cordial essence in its cell,
That in the dusky stalls, some winter's day,
  The spirit of June, here prisoned by his spell,
  May cheer the herds with pasture memories.

## Where the Cattle Come to Drink

At evening, where the cattle come to drink,
  Cool are the long marsh-grasses, dewy cool
  The alder thickets, and the shallow pool,
And the brown clay about the trodden brink.
The pensive afterthoughts of sundown sink
  Over the patient acres given to peace;
  The homely cries and farmstead noises cease,
And the worn day relaxes, link by link.

A lesson that the open heart may read
  Breathes in this mild benignity of air,
  These dear, familiar savours of the soil,—
A lesson of the calm of humble creed,
  The simple dignity of common toil,
  And the plain wisdom of unspoken prayer.


## Burnt Lands

On other fields and other scenes the morn
  Laughs from her blue,—but not such fields are these,
  Where comes no cheer of summer leaves and bees,
And no shade mitigates the day's white scorn.
These serious acres vast no groves adorn;
  But giant trunks, bleak shapes that once were trees,
  Tower naked, unassuaged of rain or breeze,
Their stern grey isolation grimly borne.

The months roll over them, and mark no change.
  But when spring stirs, or autumn stills, the year,
  Perchance some phantom leafage rustles faint
Through their parched dreams,—some old-time notes
      ring strange,
  When in his slender treble, far and clear,
  Reiterates the rain-bird his complaint.

# The Clearing

Stumps, and harsh rocks, and prostrate trunks all
    charred,
  And gnarled roots naked to the sun and rain,—
  They seem in their grim stillness to complain,
And by their plaint the evening peace is jarred.
These ragged acres fire and the axe have scarred,
  And many summers not assuaged their pain.
  In vain the pink and saffron light, in vain
The pale dew on the hillocks stripped and marred!

But here and there the waste is touched with cheer
  Where spreads the fire-weed like a crimson flood
And venturous plumes of goldenrod appear;
  And round the blackened fence the great boughs lean
With comfort; and across the solitude
  The hermit's holy transport peals serene.

# The Summer Pool

This is a wonder-cup in Summer's hand.
  Sombre, impenetrable, round its rim
  The fir-trees bend and brood. The noons o'erbrim
The windless hollow of its iris'd strand
With mote-thick sun and water-breathings bland.
  Under a veil of lilies lurk and swim
  Strange shapes of presage in a twilight dim,
Unwitting heirs of light and life's command.

Blind in their bondage, of no change they dream,
  But the trees watch in grave expectancy.
  The spell fulfils,—and swarms of radiant flame,
Live jewels, above the crystal dart and gleam,
  Nor guess the sheen beneath their wings to be
  The dark and narrow regions whence they came.

## Buckwheat

This smell of home and honey on the breeze,
  This shimmer of sunshine woven in white and pink
  That comes a dream from memory's visioned brink,
Sweet, sweet and strange across the ancient trees,—
It is the buckwheat, boon of the later bees,
  Its breadths of heavy-headed bloom appearing
  Amid the blackened stumps of this high clearing,
Freighted with cheer of comforting auguries.

But when the blunt, brown grain and red-ripe sheaves,
Brimming the low log barn beyond the eaves,
  Crisped by the first frost, feel the thresher's flail,
Then flock the blue wild-pigeons in shy haste
  All silently down Autumn's amber trail,
To glean at dawn the chill and whitening waste.


## The Cicada in the Firs

Charm of the vibrant, white September sun—
  How tower the firs to take it, tranced and still!
  Their scant ranks crown the pale, round pasture-hill,
And watch, far down, the austere waters run
Their circuit thro' the serious marshes dun.
  No bird-call stirs the blue; but strangely thrill
  The blunt-faced, brown cicada's wing-notes shrill,
A web of silver o'er the silence spun.

O zithern-winged musician, whence it came
  I wonder, this insistent song of thine!
    Did once the highest string of Summer's lyre,
Snapt on some tense chord slender as a flame,
    Take form again in these vibrations fine
      That o'er the tranquil spheres of noon aspire?

## The Potato Harvest

A high bare field, brown from the plough, and borne
    Aslant from sunset; amber wastes of sky
    Washing the ridge; a clamour of crows that fly
In from the wide flats where the spent tides mourn
To yon their rocking roosts in pines wind-torn;
    A line of grey snake-fence, that zigzags by
    A pond and cattle; from the homestead nigh
The long deep summonings of the supper horn.

Black on the ridge, against that lonely flush,
    A cart, and stoop-necked oxen; ranged beside
    Some barrels; and the day-worn harvest-folk,
Here emptying their baskets, jar the hush
    With hollow thunders.   Down the dusk hillside
    Lumbers the wain; and day fades out like smoke.

## The Oat-Threshing

A little brown old homestead, bowered in trees
    That o'er the autumn landscape shine afar,
    Burning with amber and with cinnabar.
A yellow hillside washed in airy seas
Of azure, where the swallow drops and flees.
    Midway the slope, clear in the beaming day,
    A barn by many seasons beaten grey,
Big with the gain of prospering husbandries.

In billows round the wide red welcoming doors
    High piles the golden straw; while from within,
    Where plods the team amid the chaffy din,
The loud pulsation of the thresher soars,
    Persistent as if earth could not let cease
    This happy proclamation of her peace.

## The Autumn Thistles

The morning sky is white with mist, the earth
    White with the inspiration of the dew.
    The harvest light is on the hills anew,
And cheer in the grave acres' fruitful girth.

Only in this high pasture is there dearth,
　Where the grey thistles crowd in ranks austere,
　As if the sod, close-cropt for many a year,
Brought only bane and bitterness to birth.

But in the crisp air's amethystine wave
　How the harsh stalks are washed with radiance now,
　How gleams the harsh turf where the crickets lie
Dew-freshened in their burnished armour brave!
　Since earth could not endure nor heaven allow
　Aught of unlovely in the morn's clear eye.


## The Pumpkins in the Corn

Amber and blue, the smoke behind the hill,
　Where in the glow fades out the morning star,
　Curtains the autumn cornfield, sloped afar,
And strikes an acrid savour on the chill.
The hilltop fence shines saffron o'er the still
　Unbending ranks of bunched and bleaching corn,
　And every pallid stalk is crisp with morn,
Crisp with the silver autumn morns distil.

Purple the narrowing alleys stretched between
　The spectral shooks, a purple harsh and cold,
　But spotted, where the gadding pumpkins run,
With bursts of blaze that startle the serene
　Like sudden voices,—globes of orange bold,
　Elate to mimic the unrisen sun.


## The Winter Fields

Winds here, and sleet, and frost that bites like steel.
　The low bleak hill rounds under the low sky.
　Naked of flock and fold the fallows lie,
Thin streaked with meagre drift. The gusts reveal
By fits the dim grey snakes of fence, that steal
　Through the white dusk. The hill-foot poplars sigh,
　While storm and death with winter trample by,
And the iron fields ring sharp, and blind lights reel.

Yet in the lonely ridges, wrenched with pain,
  Harsh solitary hillocks, bound and dumb,
Grave glebes close-lipped beneath the scourge and
      chain,
  Lurks hid the germ of ecstasy—the sum
Of life that waits on summer, till the rain
  Whisper in April and the crocus come.


## In An Old Barn

Tons upon tons the brown-green fragrant hay
  O'erbrims the mows beyond the time-warped eaves,
  Up to the rafters where the spider weaves,
Though few flies wander his secluded way.
Through a high chink one lonely golden ray,
  Wherein the dust is dancing, slants unstirred.
  In the dry hush some rustlings light are heard,
Of winter-hidden mice at furtive play.

Far down, the cattle in their shadowed stalls,
  Nose-deep in clover fodder's meadowy scent,
  Forget the snows that whelm their pasture streams,
The frost that bites the world beyond their walls.
  Warm housed, they dream of summer, well content
  In day-long contemplation of their dreams.


## The Stillness of the Frost

Out of the frost-white wood comes winnowing through
  No wing; no homely call or cry is heard.
  Even the hope of life seems far deferred.
The hard hills ache beneath their spectral hue.
A dove-grey cloud, tender as tears or dew,
  From one lone hearth exhaling, hangs unstirred,
  Like the poised ghost of some unnamed great bird
In the ineffable pallor of the blue.

Such, I must think, even at the dawn of Time,
  Was thy white hush, O world, when thou lay'st cold,
    Unwaked to love, new from the Maker's word,
    And the spheres, watching, stilled their high accord,
  To marvel at perfection in thy mould,
The grace of thine austerity sublime!

# VI. Miscellaneous Poems and Sonnets

## In the Wide Awe and Wisdom of the Night

In the wide awe and wisdom of the night
  I saw the round world rolling on its way,
Beyond significance of depth or height,
  Beyond the interchange of dark and day.
I marked the march to which is set no pause,
  And that stupendous orbit round whose rim
The great sphere sweeps, obedient unto laws
  That utter the eternal thought of Him.
I compassed time, outstripped the starry speed,
  And in my still Soul apprehended space,
Till, weighing laws which these but blindly heed,
  At last I came before Him face to face,—
And knew the universe of no such span
As the august infinitude of man.

## O Solitary of the Austere Sky

O Solitary of the austere sky,
  Pale presence of the unextinguished star,
That from thy station where the spheres wheel by,
  And quietudes of infinite patience are,
Watchest this wet, grey-visaged world emerge,—
  Cold pinnacle on pinnacle, and deep
On deep of ancient wood and wandering surge,—
  Out of the silence and the mists of sleep;
How small am I in thine august regard!
  Invisible,—and yet I know my worth!
When comes the hour to break this prisoning shard,
  And reunite with Him that breathed me forth,
Then shall this atom of the Eternal Soul
Encompass thee in its benign control!

## Blomidon

This is that black rock bastion, based in surge,
  Pregnant with agate and with amethyst,
Whose foot the tides of storied Minas scourge,
  Whose top austere withdraws into its mist.
This is that ancient cape of tears and storm,
  Whose towering front inviolable frowns
O'er vales Evangeline and love keep warm—
  Whose fame thy song, O tender singer, crowns.

Yonder, across these reeling fields of foam,
   Came the sad threat of the avenging ships.
What profit now to know if just the doom,
   Though harsh! The streaming eyes, the praying lips,
The shadow of inextinguishable pain,
The poet's deathless music—these remain!

## The Deserted City

There lies a little city leagues away.
   Its wharves the green sea washes all day long.
   Its busy, sun-bright wharves with sailors' song
And clamour of trade ring loud the livelong day.
Into the happy harbour hastening, gay
   With press of snowy canvas, tall ships throng.
   The peopled streets to blithe-eyed Peace belong,
Glad housed beneath these crowding roofs of grey.

'Twas long ago this city prospered so,
   For yesterday a woman died therein.
Since when the wharves are idle fallen, I know,
   And in the streets is hushed the pleasant din;
   The thronging ships have been, the songs have
      been,—
Since yesterday it is so long ago.

## Dark

Now, for the night is hushed and blind with rain,
   My soul desires communion, Dear, with thee.
   But hour by hour my spirit gets not free,—
Hour by still hour my longing strives in vain.
The thick dark hems me, ev'n to the restless brain.
   The wind's confusion vague encumbers me.
   Ev'n passionate memory, grown too faint to see
Thy features, stirs not in her straitening chain.

And thou, dost thou too feel this strange divorce
   Of will from power? The spell of night and wind,
   Baffling desire and dream, dost thou too find?
Not distance parts us, Dear; but this dim force,
   Intangible, holds us helpless, hushed with pain,
   Dumb with the dark, blind with the gusts of rain!

# Moonlight

The fifers of these amethystine fields,
　　Whose far fine sound the night makes musical,
　　Now while thou wak'st and longing would'st recall
Joys that no rapture of remembrance yields,
Voice to thy soul, lone-sitting deep within
　　The still recesses of thine ecstasy,
　　My love and my desire, that fain would fly
With this far-silvering moon and fold thee in.

But not for us the touch, the clasp, the kiss,
　　And for our restlessness no rest.　In vain
　　These aching lips, these hungering hearts that strain
Toward the denied fruition of our bliss,
　　Had love not learned of longing to devise
　　Out of desire and dream our paradise.


# Going Over

A girl's voice in the night troubled my heart.
Across the roar of the guns, the crash of the shells,
Low and soft as a sigh, clearly I heard it.

Where was the broken parapet, crumbling about me?
Where my shadowy comrades, crouching expectant?
A girl's voice in the dark troubled my heart.

A dream was the ooze of the trench, the wet clay
　　slipping;
A dream the sudden out-flare of the wide-flung Verys.
I saw but a garden of lilacs, aflower in the dusk.

What was the sergeant saying?—I passed it along.—
Did *I* pass it along?　I was breathing the breath of the
　　lilacs.
For a girl's voice in the night troubled my heart.

Over!　How the mud sucks!　Vomits red the barrage.
But I am far off in the hush of a garden of lilacs.
For a girl's voice in the night troubled my heart.
Tender and soft as a sigh, clearly I heard it.

## On the Elevated Railway at 110th Street

Above the hollow deep where lies
   The city's slumbering face,
Out, out across the night we swing,
   A meteor launched in space.

The dark above is sown with stars.
   The humming dark below
With sparkle of ten thousand lamps
   In endless row on row.

Tall shadow towers with glimmering lights
   Stand sinister and grim
Where upper deep and lower deep
   Come darkly rim to rim.

Our souls have known the midnight awe
   Of mount, and plain, and sea;
But here the city's night enfolds
   A vaster mystery.

## At Tide Water

The red and yellow of the Autumn salt-grass,
   The grey flats, and the yellow-grey full tide,
The lonely stacks, the grave expanse of marshes,—
   O Land wherein my memories abide,
I have come back that you may make me tranquil,
   Resting a little at your heart of peace,
Remembering much amid your serious leisure,
   Forgetting more amid your large release.
For yours the wisdom of the night and morning,
   The word of the inevitable years,
The open heaven's unobscured communion,
   And the dim whisper of the wheeling spheres.
The great things and the terrible I bring you,
   To be illumined in your spacious breath,—
Love, and the ashes of desire, and anguish,
   Strange laughter, and the unhealing wound of death.
These in the world, all these, have come upon me,
   Leaving me mute and shaken with surprise.
Oh, turn them in your measureless contemplation,
   And in their mastery teach me to be wise.

[ 114 ]

## All Night the Lone Cicada

All night the lone cicada
 Kept shrilling through the rain,
A voice of joy undaunted
 By unforgotten pain.

Down from the tossing branches
 Rang out the high refrain,
By tumult undisheartened,
 By storm assailed in vain.

To looming vasts of mountain,
 To shadowy deeps of plain
The ephemeral, brave defiance
 Adventured not in vain,—

Till to my faltering spirit,
 And to my weary brain,
From loss and fear and failure
 My joy returned again.


## Night in a Down-Town Street

Not in the eyed, expectant gloom,
 Where soaring peaks repose
And incommunicable space
 Companions with the snows;

Not in the glimmering dusk that crawls
 Upon the clouded sea,
Where bourneless wave on bourneless wave
 Complains continually;

Not in the palpable dark of woods
 Where groping hands clutch fear,
Does Night her deeps of solitude
 Reveal unveiled as here.

The street is a grim cañon carved
 In the eternal stone,
That knows no more the rushing stream
 It anciently has known.

The emptying tide of life has drained
  The iron channel dry.
Strange winds from the forgotten day
  Draw down, and dream, and sigh.

The narrow heaven, the desolate moon
  Made wan with endless years,
Seem less immeasurably remote
  Than laughter, love, or tears.


## Eastward Bound

We mount the arc of ocean's round
  To meet the splendours of the sun;
Then downward rush into the dark
  When the blue, spacious day is done.

The slow, eternal drift of stars
  Draws over us until the dawn,
Then the grey steep we mount once more,
  And night is down the void withdrawn.

Space, and interminable hours,
  And moons that rise, and sweep, and fall,—
On-swinging earth, and orbèd sea,—
  And voyaging souls more vast than all!


## A Wake-up Song

Sun's up; wind's up!  Wake up, dearies!
  Leave your coverlets white and downy.
June's come into the world this morning.
  Wake up, Golden Head!  Wake up, Brownie!

Dew on the meadow-grass, waves on the water,
  Robins in the rowan-tree wondering about you!
Don't keep the buttercups so long waiting.
  Don't keep the bobolinks singing without you.

Wake up, Golden Head!  Wake up, Brownie!
  Cat-bird wants you in the garden soon.
You and I, butterflies, bobolinks, and clover,
  We've a lot to do on the first of June.

## The Piper and the Chiming Peas

There was a little piper man
As merry as you please,
Who heard one day the sweet-pea blossoms
Chiming in the breeze.

He murmured with a courtly grace
That set them quite at ease,—
"I never knew that you had such
Accomplishments as these!

"If I should pipe until you're ripe
I think that by degrees
You might become as wise as I
And chime in Wagnerese!"

"Oh, no, kind Sir! That could not be!"
Replied the modest peas.
"We only play such simple airs
As suit the bumble-bees."

## Heat in the City

Over the scorching roofs of iron
The red moon rises slow.
Uncomforted beneath its light
The pale crowds gasping go.

The heart-sick city, spent with day,
Cries out in vain for sleep.
The childless wife beside her dead
Is too outworn to weep.

The children in the upper rooms
Lie faint, with half-shut eyes.
In the thick-breathing, lighted ward
The stricken workman dies.

From breathless pit and sweltering loft
Dim shapes creep one by one
To throng the curb and crowd the stoops
And fear to-morrow's sun.

[ 117 ]

## When the Clover Blooms Again

"When the clover blooms again,
    And the rain-birds in the rain
        Make the sad-heart noon seem sweeter
        And the joy of June completer,
    I shall see his face again!"

Of her lover over sea
So she whispered happily;
    And she prayed, while men were sleeping,
    "Mary, have him in thy keeping
As he sails the stormy sea!"

White and silent lay his face
In a still, green-watered place,
    Where the long, grey weed scarce lifted,
    And the sand was lightly sifted
O'er his unremembering face.

## Twilight on Sixth Avenue at Ninth Street

Over the tops of the houses
    Twilight and sunset meet.
The green, diaphanous dusk
    Sinks to the eager street.

Astray in the tangle of roofs
    Wanders a wind of June.
The dial shines in the clock-tower
    Like the face of a strange-scrawled moon.

The narrowing lines of the houses
    Palely begin to gleam,
And the hurrying crowds fade softly
    Like an army in a dream.

Above the vanishing faces
    A phantom train flares on
With a voice that shakes the shadows,—
    Diminishes, and is gone.

And I walk with the journeying throng
    In such a solitude
As where a lonely ocean
    Washes a lonely wood.

# The Wrestler

When God sends out His company to travel through
    the stars,
  There is every kind of wonder in the show;
There is every kind of animal behind its prison bars;
  With riders in a many-coloured row.
The master showman, Time, has a strange trick of
    rhyme,
  And the clown's most ribald jest is a tear;
But the best drawing card is the Wrestler huge and
    hard,
  Who can fill the tent at any time of year.

His eye is on the crowd and he beckons with his hand,
  With authoritative finger, and they come.
The rules of the game they do not understand,
  But they go as in a dream, and are dumb.
They would fain say him nay, and they look the
    other way,
  Till at last to the ropes they cling.
But he throws them one by one till the show for them
    is done,
  In the blood-red dust of the ring.

There's none to shun his challenge—they must meet
    him soon or late,
  And he knows a cunning trick for all heels.
The king's haughty crown drops in jeers from his pate
  As the hold closes on him, and he reels.
The burly and the proud, the braggarts of the crowd,
  Every one of them he topples down in thunder.
His grip grows mild for the dotard and the child,
  But alike they must all go under.

Oh, many a mighty foeman would try a fall with him;—
  Persepolis, and Babylon, and Rome,
Assyria and Sardis, they see their fame grow dim
  As he tumbles in the dust every dome.
At last will come an hour when the stars shall feel his
    power,
  And he shall have his will upon the sun.
Ere we know what he's about the lights will be put out,
  And the wonder of the show will be undone.

## Soliloquy in a Monastery

Cuthbert, open!  Let me in!
   Cease your praying for a minute!
Here the darkness seems to grin,
   Holds a thousand horrors in it.
Down the stony corridor
Footsteps pace the stony floor.

Here they foot it, pacing slow,
   Monk-like, one behind another!—
Don't you hear me?  Don't you know
   I'm a little nervous, Brother?
Won't you speak?  Then, by your leave,
Here 's a guest for Christmas Eve!

Shrive me, but I got a fright!
   Monks of centuries ago
Wander back to see to-night
   How the old place looks—Hello!
This the kind of watch you keep!
Come to pray—and go to sleep!

Ah, this mortal flesh is weak!
   Who is saintly there 's no saying.
Here are tears upon his cheek,
   And he sleeps that should be praying;—
Sleeps, and dreams, and murmurs.  Nay,
I'll not wake you.—Sleep away!

Holy saints, the night is keen!
   How the nipping wind does drive
Through yon tree-tops, bare and lean,
   Till their shadow seems alive,—
Patters through the bars, and falls,
Shivering, on the floor and walls!

How yon patch of freezing sky
   Echoes back their bell-ringings!
Down in the grey city, nigh
   Severn, every steeple swings.
All the busy streets are bright.
Many folk are out to-night.

—What's that, Brother?   Did you speak?—
   Christ save them that talk in sleep!
Smile they howsoever meek,
   Somewhat in their hearts they keep.
*We*, good souls, what shifts we make
To keep talking whilst awake!

Christ be praised, that fetched me in
   Early, yet a youngling, while
All unlearned in life and sin,
   Love and travail, grief and guile!
For your world of two-score years,
Cuthbert, all you have is tears.

Dreaming, still he hears the bells
   As he heard them years ago,
Ere he sought our quiet cells
   Iron-mouthed and wrenched with woe,
Out of what dread storms who knows—
Faithfulest of friends and foes!

Faithful was he aye, I ween,
   Pitiful, and kind, and wise;
But in mindful moods I've seen
   Flame enough in those sunk eyes!
Praised be Christ, whose timely hand
Plucked from out the fire this brand!

Now in dreams he 's many miles
   Hence, he 's back in Ireland.
Ah, how tenderly he smiles,
   Stretching a caressing hand!
Backward now his memory glides
To old, happy Christmastides.

Now once more a loving wife
   Holds him; now he sees his boys,
Smiles at all their playful strife,
   All their childish mirth and noise;
Softly now she strokes his hair.—
Ah, their world is very fair!

—Waking, all your loss shall be
   Unforgotten evermore!
Sleep alone holds these for thee.
   Sleep then, Brother!—To restore
All your heaven that has died
Heaven and Hell may be too wide!

Sleep, and dream, and be awhile
   Happy, Cuthbert, once again!
Soon you'll wake, and cease to smile,
   And your heart will sink with pain.
You will hear the merry town,—
And a weight will press you down.

Hungry-hearted you will see
   Only the thin shadows fall
From yon bleak-topped poplar-tree,—
   Icy fingers on the wall.
You will watch them come and go,
Telling o'er your count of woe.

—Nay, now, hear me, how I prate!
   I, a foolish monk, and old,
Maundering o'er a life and fate
   To me unknown, by you untold!
Yet I know you're like to weep
Soon, so, Brother, this night sleep.


## A Child's Prayer at Evening

*(Domine, cui sunt Pleiades curae)*

Father, who keepest
   The stars in Thy care,
Me, too, Thy little one,
   Childish in prayer,
Keep, as Thou keepest
The soft night through,
Thy long, white lilies
   Asleep in Thy dew.


[ 122 ]

# VII.  Patriotic Poems

## Collect for Dominion Day

Father of nations! Help of the feeble hand!
    Strength of the strong! to whom the nations kneel!
Stay and destroyer, at whose just command
    Earth's kingdoms tremble and her empires reel!
Who dost the low uplift, the small make great,
    And dost abase the ignorantly proud,
Of our scant people mould a mighty state,
    To the strong, stern,—to Thee in meekness bowed!
Father of unity, make this people one!
    Weld, interfuse them in the patriot's flame,—
Whose forging on thine anvil was begun
    In blood late shed to purge the common shame;
That so our hearts, the fever of faction done,
    Banish old feud in our young nation's name.

## Canada

O Child of Nations, giant-limbed,
    Who stand'st among the nations now
Unheeded, unadored, unhymned,
    With unanointed brow,—

How long the ignoble sloth, how long
    The trust in greatness not thine own?
Surely the lion's brood is strong
    To front the world alone!

How long the indolence, ere thou dare
    Achieve thy destiny, seize thy fame,—
Ere our proud eyes behold thee bear
    A nation's franchise, nation's name?

The Saxon force, the Celtic fire,
    These are thy manhood's heritage!
Why rest with babes and slaves? Seek higher
    The place of race and age.

I see to every wind unfurled
    The flag that bears the Maple Wreath;
Thy swift keels furrow round the world
    Its blood-red folds beneath;

[ 125 ]

Thy swift keels cleave the furthest seas;
  Thy white sails swell with alien gales;
To stream on each remotest breeze
  The black smoke of thy pipes exhales.

O Falterer, let thy past convince
  Thy future,—all the growth, the gain,
The fame since Cartier knew thee, since
  Thy shores beheld Champlain!

Montcalm and Wolfe! Wolfe and Montcalm!
  Quebec, thy storied citadel
Attest in burning song and psalm
  How here thy heroes fell!

O Thou that bor'st the battle's brunt
  At Queenston and at Lundy's Lane,—
On whose scant ranks but iron front
  The battle broke in vain!—

Whose was the danger, whose the day,
  From whose triumphant throats the cheers,
At Chrysler's Farm, at Chateauguay,
  Storming like clarion-bursts our ears?

On soft Pacific slopes,—beside
  Strange floods that northward rave and fall,—
Where chafes Acadia's chainless tide—
  Thy sons await thy call.

They wait; but some in exile, some
  With strangers housed, in stranger lands,—
And some Canadian lips are dumb
  Beneath Egyptian sands.

O mystic Nile! Thy secret yields
  Before us; thy most ancient dreams
Are mixed with far Canadian fields
  And murmur of Canadian streams.

But thou, my country, dream not thou!
  Wake, and behold how night is done,—
How on thy breast, and o'er thy brow,
  Bursts the uprising sun!

## Canadian Streams

O rivers rolling to the sea
From lands that bear the maple-tree,
  How swell your voices with the strain
Of loyalty and liberty!

A holy music, heard in vain
By coward heart and sordid brain,
  To whom this strenuous being seems
Naught but a greedy race for gain.

O unsung streams—not splendid themes
Ye lack to fire your patriot dreams!
  Annals of glory gild your waves,
Hope freights your tides, Canadian streams!

St. Lawrence, whose wide water laves
The shores that ne'er have nourished slaves!
  Swift Richelieu of lilied fame!
Niagara of glorious graves!

Thy rapids, Ottawa, proclaim
Where Daulac and his heroes came!
  Thy tides, St. John, declare La Tour,
And, later, many a loyal name!

Thou inland stream, whose vales, secure
From storm, Tecumseh's death made poor!
  And thou small water, red with war,
'Twixt Beaubassin and Beauséjour!

Dread Saguenay, where eagles soar,
What voice shall from the bastioned shore
  The tale of Roberval reveal,
Or his mysterious fate deplore?

Annapolis, do thy floods yet feel
Faint memories of Champlain's keel,
  Thy pulses yet the deeds repeat
Of Poutrincourt and D'Iberville?

And thou far tide, whose plains now beat
With march of myriad westering feet,
  Saskatchewan, whose virgin sod
So late Canadian blood made sweet?

Your bulwark hills, your valleys broad,
Streams where De Salaberry trod,
  Where Wolfe achieved, where Brock was slain,—
Your voices are the voice of God!

O sacred waters! not in vain,
Across Canadian height and plain,
  Ye sound us in triumphant tone
The summons of your high refrain.


## Jonathan and John

Should Jonathan and John fall out
The world would stagger from that bout.
With John and Jonathan at one
The world's great peace will have begun.

With Jonathan and John at war
The hour that havoc  hungers for
Will strike, in ruin of blood and tears,—
The world set back a thousand years.

With John and Jonathan sworn to stand
Shoulder to shoulder, hand by hand,
Justice and peace shall build their throne
From tropic sea to frozen zone.

When Jonathan and John forget
The scar of an ancient wound to fret
And smile to think of an ancient feud
Which the God of the nations turned to good;

When the bond of a common creed and speech
And kindred binds them each to each,
And each in the other's victories
The pride of his own achievement sees,—

How paltry a thing they both will know
That grudge of a hundred years ago,—
How small that blemish of wrath and blame
In the blazonry of their common fame!

[ 128 ]

# VIII. Ballads

# How the Mohawks Set Out for Medoctec

[*When the invading Mohawks captured the outlying Melicite village of Madawaska, they spared two squaws to guide them downstream to the main Melicite town of Medoctec, below Grand Falls. The squaws steered themselves and their captors over the Falls.*]

### I

Grows the great deed, though none
Shout to behold it done!
To the brave deed done by night
Heaven testifies in the light.

Stealthy and swift as a dream,
Crowding the breast of the stream,
In their paint and plumes of war
And their war-canoes four score,

They are threading the Oolastook,
Where his cradling hills o'erlook.
The branchy thickets hide them;
The unstartled waters guide them.

### II

Comes night to the quiet hills
Where the Madawaska spills,—
To his slumbering huts no warning,
Nor mirth of another morning!

No more shall the children wake
As the dawns through the hut-door break;
But the dogs, a trembling pack,
With wistful eyes steal back.

And, to pilot the noiseless foe
Through the perilous passes, go
Two women who could not die—
Whom the knife in the dark passed by.

### III

Where the shoaling waters froth,
Churned thick like devils' broth,—
Where the rocky shark-jaw waits,
Never a bark that grates.

[ 131 ]

And the tearless captives' skill
Contents them.   Onward still!
And the low-voiced captives tell
The tidings that cheer them well;

How a clear stream leads them down
Well-nigh to Medoctec town,
Ere to the great Falls' thunder
The long wall yawns asunder.

IV

The clear stream glimmers before them;
The faint night falters o'er them;
Lashed lightly bark to bark,
They glide the windless dark.

Late grows the night.   No fear
While the skilful captives steer!
Sleeps the tired warrior, sleeps
The chief; and the river creeps.

V

In the town of the Melicite
The unjarred peace is sweet,
Green grows the corn and great,
And the hunt is fortunate.

This many a heedless year
The Mohawks come not near.
The lodge-gate stands unbarred;
Scarce even a dog keeps guard.

No mother shrieks from a dream
Of blood on the threshold stream,—
But the thought of those mute guides
Is where the sleeper bides!

VI

Gets forth those caverned walls
No roar from the giant Falls,
Whose mountainous foam treads under
The abyss of awful thunder.

But the river's sudden speed!
How the ghost-grey shores recede!
And the tearless pilots hear
A muttering voice creep near.

A tremor! The blanched waves leap.
The warriors start from sleep.
Faints in the sudden blare
The cry of their swift despair,

And the captives' death-chant shrills.
But afar, remote from ills,
Quiet under the quiet skies
The Melicite village lies.


## The Stranded Ship

Far up the lonely strand the storm had lifted her.
And now along her keel the merry tides make stir
No more. The running waves that sparkled at her
    prow
Seethe to the chains and sing no more with laughter
    now.
No more the clean sea-furrow follows her. No more.
To the hum of her gallant tackle the hale Nor'-westers
    roar.
No more her bulwarks journey. For the only boon
    they crave
Is the guerdon of all good ships and true, the boon of
    a deep-sea grave.

*Take me out, sink me deep in the green profound,*
*To sway with the long weed, swing with the drowned,*
*Where the change of the soft tide makes no sound,*
*Far below the keels of the outward bound.*

No more she mounts the circles from Fundy to the
    Horn,
From Cuba to the Cape runs down the tropic morn,
Explores the Vast Uncharted where great bergs ride
    in ranks,
Nor shouts a broad "Ahoy" to the dories on the Banks.

No more she races freights to Zanzibar and back,
Nor creeps where the fog lies blind along the liners'
track.
No more she dares the cyclone's disastrous core of
calm
To greet across the dropping wave the amber isles of
palm.

*Take me out, sink me deep in the green profound,*
*To sway with the long weed, swing with the drowned,*
*Where the change of the soft tide makes no sound,*
*Far below the keels of the outward bound.*

Amid her trafficking peers, the wind-wise, journeyed
ships,
At the black wharves no more, nor at the weedy slips,
She comes to port with cargo from many a storied
clime.
No more to the rough-throat chantey her windlass
creaks in time.
No more she loads for London with spices from
Ceylon,—
With white spruce deals and wheat and apples from
St. John.
No more from Pernambuco with coffee-bags,—no more
With hides from Buenos Ayres she clears for Baltimore.

*Take me out, sink me deep in the green profound,*
*To sway with the long weed, swing with the drowned,*
*Where the change of the soft tide makes no sound,*
*Far below the keels of the outward bound.*

Wan with the slow vicissitudes of wind and rain and
sun
How grieves her deck for the sailors whose hearty
brawls are done!
Only the wandering gull brings word of the open wave,
With shrill scream at her taffrail deriding her alien
grave.
Around the keel that raced the dolphin and the shark
Only the sand-wren twitters from barren dawn till
dark;

And all the long blank noon the blank sand chafes
and mars
The prow once swift to follow the lure of the dancing
stars.

*Take me out, sink me deep in the green profound,*
*To sway with the long weed, swing with the drowned,*
*Where the change of the soft tide makes no sound,*
*Far below the keels of the outward bound.*

And when the winds are low, and when the tides are
still,
And the round moon rises inland over the naked hill,
And o'er her parching seams the dry cloud-shadows
pass,
And dry along the land-rim lie the shadows of thin
grass,
Then aches her soul with longing to launch and sink
away
Where the fine silts lift and settle, the sea-things drift
and stray,
To make the port of Last Desire, and slumber with
her peers
In the tide-wash rocking softly through the unnumbered
years.

*Take me out, sink me deep in the green profound,*
*To sway with the long weed, swing with the drowned,*
*Where the change of the soft tide makes no sound,*
*Far below the keels of the outward bound.*


## The Laughing Sally

A wind blew up from Pernambuco.
    (Yeo heave ho! the *Laughing Sally!*
      Hi yeo, heave away!)
A wind blew out of the east-sou'-east
And boomed at the break of day.

The *Laughing Sally* sped for her life,
    And a speedy craft was she.
The black flag flew at her top to tell
    How she took toll of the sea.

The wind blew up from Pernambuco;
  And in the breast of the blast
Came the King's black ship like a hound let slip
  On the trail of the *Sally* at last.

For a day and a night, a night and a day,
  Over the blue, blue round,
Went on the chase of the pirate quarry,
  The hunt of the tireless hound.

"Land on the port bow!" came the cry;
  And the *Sally* raced for shore,
Till she reached the bar at the river-mouth
  Where the shallow breakers roar.

She passed the bar by a secret channel
  With clear tide under her keel,—
For he knew the shoals like an open book,
  The captain at the wheel.

She passed the bar, she sped like a ghost,
  Till her sails were hid from view
By the tall, liana'd, unsunned boughs
  O'erbrooding the dark bayou.

At moonrise up to the river-mouth
  Came the King's black ship of war.
The red cross flapped in wrath at her peak,
  But she could not cross the bar.

And while she lay in the run of the seas,
  By the grimmest whim of chance
Out of the bay to the north came forth
  Two battle-ships of France.

On the English ship the twain bore down
  Like wolves that range by night;
And the breakers' roar was heard no more
  In the thunder of the fight.

The crash of the broadsides rolled and stormed
  To the *Sally*, hid from view
Under the tall, liana'd boughs
  Of the moonless, dark bayou.

A boat ran out for news of the fight,
    And this was the word she brought—
"The King's ship fights the ships of France
    As the King's ships all have fought!"

Then muttered the mate, "I'm a man of Devon!"
    And the captain thundered then—
"There's English rope that bides for our necks,
    But we all be English men!"

The *Sally* glided out of the gloom
    And down the moon-white river.
She stole like a grey shark over the bar
    Where the long surf seethes forever.

She hove to under a high French hull,
    And the red cross rose to her peak.
The French were looking for fight that night,
    And they had not far to seek.

Blood and fire on the streaming decks,
    And fire and blood below;
The heat of hell, and the reek of hell,
    And the dead men laid a-row!

And when the stars paled out of heaven
    And the red dawn-rays uprushed,
The oaths of battle, the crash of timbers,
    The roar of the guns were hushed.

With one foe beaten under his bow,
    The other afar in flight,
The English captain turned to look
    For his fellow in the fight.

The English captain turned, and stared;—
    For where the *Sally* had been
Was a single spar upthrust from the sea
    With the red-cross flag serene!

       *       *       *       *       *

A wind blew up from Pernambuco,—
    (Yeo heave ho! the *Laughing Sally*!
    Hi yeo, heave away!)
And boomed for the doom of the *Laughing Sally*,
    Gone down at the break of day.

[ 137 ]

## The Muse and the Wheel

The poet took his wheel one day
  A-wandering to go,
But soon fell out beside the way,
  The leaves allured him so.

He leaned his wheel against a tree
  And in the shade lay down;
And more to him were bloom and bee
  Than all the busy town.

He listened to the Phoebe-bird
  And learned a thing worth knowing.
He lay so still he almost heard
  The merry grasses growing.

He lay so still he dropped asleep;
  And then the Muse came by.
The stars were in her garment's sweep
  But laughter in her eye.

"Poor boy!" she said, "how tired he seems!
  His vagrant feet must follow
So many loves, so many dreams,—
  (To find them mostly hollow!)

"No marvel if he does not feel
  My old familiar nearness!"
And then her gaze fell on his wheel
  And wondered at its queerness.

"Can you be Pegasus," she mused,
  "To modern mood translated,
But poorly housed, and meanly used,
  And grown attenuated?

"Ah, no, you're quite another breed
  From him who once would follow
Across the clear Olympian mead
  The calling of Apollo!

"No Hippocrene would leap to light
  If you should stamp your hoof.
You never knew the pastures bright
  Wherein we lie aloof.

[ 138 ]

"You never drank of Helicon,
    Or strayed in Tempe's vale.
You never soared against the sun
    Till earth grew faint and pale.

"You bear my poor deluded boy
    Each latest love to see!
But Pegasus would mount with joy
    And bring him straight to me!"

He woke. The olden spell was strong
    Within his eager bosom,
And so he wrote a mystic song
    Upon the nearest blossom.

He wrote, until a sudden whim
    Set all his bosom trembling;
Then sped to woo a maiden slim
    His latest love resembling.


## The Ballad of Crossing the Brook

Oh, it was a dainty maid that went a-Maying in the
    morn,
    A dainty, dainty maiden of degree.
The ways she took were merry and the ways she
    missed forlorn,
    And the laughing water tinkled to the sea.

The little leaves above her loved the dainty, dainty
    maid;
    The little winds they kissed her, every one.
At the nearing of her little feet the flowers were not
    afraid;
    And the water lay a-whimpling in the sun.

Oh, the dainty, dainty maid to the borders of the
    brook
    Lingered down as lightly as the breeze;
And the shy water-spiders quit their scurrying to look;
    And the happy water whispered to the trees.

[ 139 ]

She was fain to cross the brook, was the dainty, dainty
    maid;
  But first she lifted up her elfin eyes
To see if there were cavalier or clown a-near to aid,—
  And the water-bubbles blinked in surprise.

The brook bared its pebbles to persuade her dainty
    feet,
  But the dainty, dainty maid was not content.
She had spied a simple country lad (for dainty maid
    unmeet),
  And the sly water twinkled as it went.

As the simple lad drew nigh, then this dainty, dainty
    maid,
  (O maidens, well you know how it was done!)
Stood a-gazing at her feet until he saw she was afraid
  Of the water there a-whimpling in the sun.

Now that simple lad had in him all the makings of a
    man;
  And he stammered, "I had better lift you over!"
Said the dainty, dainty maid—"Do you really think
    you can?"
  And the water hid its laughter in the clover.

So he carried her across, with his eyes cast down,
  And his foolish heart a-quaking with delight.
And the maid she looked him over with her elfin eyes
    of brown;
  And the impish water giggled at his plight.

He reached the other side, he set down the dainty maid;
  But he trembled so he couldn't speak a word.
Then the dainty, dainty maid—"Thank you, Sir!
    Good-day!" she said.
  And the water-bubbles chuckled as they heard.

Oh, she tripped away so lightly, a-Maying in the
    morn,
  That dainty, dainty maiden of degree.
She left the simple country lad a-sighing and forlorn
  Where the mocking water twinkled to the sea.

# IX. Epitaphs and Elegies

# Epitaph for a Sailor Buried Ashore

He who but yesterday would roam
　　Careless as clouds and currents range,
In homeless wandering most at home,
　　Inhabiter of change;

Who wooed the west to win the east,
　　And named the stars of North and South,
And felt the zest of Freedom's feast
　　Familiar in his mouth;

Who found a faith in stranger speech,
　　And fellowship in foreign hands,
And had within his eager reach
　　The relish of all lands—

How circumscribed a plot of earth
　　Keeps now his restless footsteps still,
Whose wish was wide as ocean's girth,
　　Whose will the water's will!


# An Epitaph for a Husbandman

He who would start and rise
　　Before the crowing cocks,—
No more he lifts his eyes,
　　Whoever knocks.

He who before the stars
　　Would call the cattle home,—
They wait about the bars
　　For him to come.

Him at whose hearty calls
　　The farmstead woke again
The horses in their stalls
　　Expect in vain.

Busy and blithe and bold
　　He laboured for the morrow,—
The plough his hands would hold
　　Rusts in the furrow.

[ 143 ]

His fields he had to leave,
   His orchards cool and dim;
The clods he used to cleave
   Now cover him.

But the green, growing things
   Lean kindly to his sleep,—
White roots and wandering strings,
   Closer they creep.

Because he loved them long
   And with them bore his part,
Tenderly now they throng
   About his heart.

## Epitaph for a Certain Architect

His fame the mock of shallow wits,
His name the jest of fool and child,
Remains the dream he fixed in form,
Remains the stone he hewed and piled.

Untouched by scorn that dogged his way
Ere the great task was well begun,
He drudged to give the vision life
And died content when it was done.

They pass, the mockers, and are dust,
While stars conspire to enscroll his name.
When roaring guns are fallen to rust
This granite shall attest his fame.

Eternal as the returning rose,
Impregnable as the perfect rhyme,
Through the long sequence of the suns
His dream in stone shall outwear Time.

## The Valley of the Winding Water

The valley of the winding water
   Wears the same light it wore of old.
Still o'er the purple peaks the portals
   Of distance and desire unfold.

Still break the fields of opening June
  To emerald in their ancient way.
The sapphire of the summer heaven
  Is infinite, as yesterday.

My eyes are on the greening earth,
  The exultant bobolinks wild awing;
And yet, of all this kindly gladness,
  My heart beholds not anything.

For in a still room far away,
  With mourners round her silent head,
Blind to the quenchless tears, the anguish—
  I see, to-day, a woman dead.


## The Little Field of Peace

By the long wash of his ancestral sea
He sleeps how quietly!
How quiet the unlifting eyelids lie
Under this tranquil sky!
The little busy hands and restless feet
Here find that rest is sweet;
For sweetly, from the hands grown tired of play,
The child-world slips away,
With its confusion of forgotten toys
And kind, familiar noise.

Not lonely does he lie in his last bed,
For love o'erbroods his head.
Kindly to him the comrade grasses lean
Their fellowship of green.
The wilding meadow companies give heed,—
Brave tansy, and the weed
That on the dyke-top lifts its dauntless stalk,—
Around his couch they talk.
The shadows of his oak-tree flit and play
Above his dreams all day.
The wind, that was his playmate on the hills,
His sleep with music fills.

Here in this tender acre by the tide
His vanished kin abide.
Ah! what compassionate care for him they keep,
Too soon returned to sleep!
They watch him in this little field of peace
Where they have found release.
Not as a stranger or alone he went
Unto his long content;
But kissed to sleep and comforted lies he
By his ancestral sea.

## The Place of His Rest*

The green marsh-mallows
    Are over him.
Along the shallows
    The pale lights swim.

Wide air, washed grasses,
    And waveless stream;
And over him passes
    The drift of dream;—

The pearl-hue down
    Of the poplar seed;
The elm-flower brown;
    And the sway of the reed;

The blue moth, winged
    With a flake of sky;
The bee, gold ringed;
    And the dragon-fly.

Lightly the rushes
    Lean to his breast;
A bird's wing brushes
    The place of his rest.

The far-flown swallow,
    The gold-finch flame,—
They come, they follow
    The paths he came.

*This poem was composed in my sleep.—C. G. D. R.

'Tis the land of No Care
   Where now he lies,
Fulfilled the prayer
   Of his weary eyes,

And while around him
   The kind grass creeps,
Where peace hath found him
   How sound he sleeps.

Well to his slumber
   Attends the year:
Soft rains without number
   Soft noons, blue clear,

With nights of balm,
   And the dark, sweet hours
Brooding with calm,
   Pregnant with flowers.

See how she speeds them,
   Each childlike bloom,
And softly leads them
   To tend his tomb!—

The white-thorn nears
   As the cowslip goes;
Then the iris appears;
   And then, the rose.

## To G. B. R.

How merry sings the aftermath,
   With crickets fifing in the dew!
The home-sweet sounds, the scene, the hour,
   I consecrate to you.

All this you knew and loved with me;
   All this in our delight had part;
And now—though us earth sees no more
   As comrades, heart to heart—

This kindly strength of open fields,
   This faith of eve, this calm of air,
They lift my spirit close to you
   In memory and prayer.

## Grey Rocks and the Greyer Sea

Grey rocks, and greyer sea,
   And surf along the shore—
And in my heart a name
   My lips shall speak no more.

The high and lonely hills
   Endure the darkening year—
And in my heart endure
   A memory and a tear.

Across the tide a sail
   That tosses, and is gone—
And in my heart the kiss
   That longing dreams upon.

Grey rocks, and greyer sea,
   And surf along the shore—
And in my heart the face
   That I shall see no more.

## New Dead

Where are the kind eyes gone
That watched me so?
Was it but now they wept,
Or long ago?

Why did they run with tears
And yearn to me?
What was it in my face
They feared to see?

Ah, world, when did I pass
Beyond your smile,—
Forget you, for a long
Or little while?

Descending from the sun
Into this night,—
Impenetrable dark
That chokes my sight,—

Ah, now I know why stirs
No more my breath!
My mouth is stopt with dust,
My dream with death.

Where is this seed of self
I clutch to hold?
Will it dissolve with me
Into the mould?

It slips,—ah, let me sleep,
Worn, worn, outworn!
So to be strong when I
Arise, new born!


## An Evening Communion

The large first stars come out
    Above the open hill,
And in the west the light
    Is lingering still.

The wide and tranquil air
    Of evening washes cool
On open hill, and vale,
    And shining pool.

The calm of endless time
    Is in the spacious hour
Whose mystery unfolds
    To perfect flower.

The silence and my heart
    Expect a voice I know,—
A voice we have not heard
    Since long ago.

Since long ago thy face,
    Thy smile, I may not see,
True comrade, whom the veil
    Divides from me.

[ 149 ]

But when earth's hidden word
   I almost understand,
I dream that on my lips
   I feel thy hand.

Thy presence is the light
   Upon the open hill.
Thou walkest with me here,
   True comrade still.

My pain and my unrest
   Thou tak'st into thy care.
The world becomes a dream,
   And life a prayer.


## Oh, Purple Hang the Pods!

Oh, purple hang the pods
   On the green locust-tree,
And yellow turn the sods
   On a grave that's dear to me!

And blue, softly blue,
   The hollow autumn sky,
With its birds flying through
   To where the sun-lands lie!

In the sun-lands they'll bide
   While winter's on the tree;—
And oh, that I might hide
   The grave that's dear to me!


## The Bird's Song, the Sun, and the Wind

The bird's song, the sun, and the wind—
   The wind that rushes, the sun that is still,
The song of the bird that sings alone,
   And wide light washing the lonely hill!

The spring's coming, the buds and the brooks—
   The brooks that clamour, the buds in the rain,
The coming of spring that comes unprayed for,
   And eyes that welcome it not for pain!

# X. Quatrains and Epigrams

## O Thou Who Bidd'st

O Thou who bidd'st a million germs decay
That one white bloom may soar into the day,
Mine eyes unseal to see their souls in death
Borne back to Thee upon the lily's breath.

## Immanence

Not only in the cataract and the thunder,
 Or in the deeps of man's uncharted soul,
But in the dew-star dwells alike the wonder,
 And in the whirling dust-mote the control.

## The Banquet

Though o'er the board the constellations shine,
 Austere the feast for Time's retainers spread,—
Laughter the salt of life, and love the wine,
 Sleep the sweet herbs, and toil the gritty bread.

## The Stirrup Cup

Life at my stirrup lifted wistful eyes,
 And as she gave the parting cup to me,—
 Death's pale companion for the silent sea,—
"I know," she said, "that land and where it lies.
 A pledge between us now before you go,
 That when you meet me there your soul may
 know!"

## The Street Lamps

 Eyes of the city,
Keeping your sleepless watch from sun to sun,
 Is it for pity
You tremble, seeing innocence undone;
 Or do you laugh, to think men thus should set
 Spies on the folly day would fain forget?

[ 153 ]

## The Frosted Pane

One night came Winter noiselessly, and leaned
   Against my window-pane.
In the deep stillness of his heart convened
   The ghosts of all his slain.

Leaves, and ephemera, and stars of earth,
   And fugitives of grass,—
White spirits loosed from bonds of mortal birth,
   He drew them on the glass.

## Life and Art

Said Life to Art—"I love thee best
   Not when I find in thee
My very face and form, expressed
   With dull fidelity,

"But when in thee my craving eyes
   Behold continually
The mystery of my memories
   And all I long to be."

## The Lily of the Valley

Did Winter, letting fall in vain regret
   A tear among the tender leaves of May,
Embalm the tribute, lest she might forget,
   In this elect, imperishable way?

Or did the virgin Spring sweet vigil keep
   In the white radiance of the midnight hour,
And whisper to the unwondering ear of sleep
   Some shy desire that turned into a flower?

## The Wild Rose Thicket

Where humming flies frequent, and where
Pink petals open to the air,

The wild-rose thicket seems to be
The summer in epitome.

Amid its gold-green coverts meet
The late dew and the noonday heat;

Around it, to the sea-rim harsh,
The patient levels of the marsh;

And o'er it the pale heavens bent,
Half sufferance and half content.


## Ice

When Winter scourged the meadow and the hill
And in the withered leafage worked his will,
The water shrank, and shuddered, and stood still,—
Then built himself a magic house of glass,
Irised with memories of flowers and grass,
Wherein to sit and watch the fury pass.


## When the Cloud Comes Down the Mountain

When the cloud comes down the mountain,
    And the rain is loud on the leaves,
And the slim flies gather for shelter
    Under my cabin eaves,—

Then my heart goes out to earth,
    With the swollen brook runs free,
Drinks life with the drenched brown roots,
    And climbs with the sap in the tree.

# Butterflies

Once in a garden, when the thrush's song,
  Pealing at morn, made holy all the air,
Till earth was healed of many an ancient wrong,
  And life appeared another name for prayer,

Rose suddenly a swarm of butterflies,
  On wings of white and gold and azure fire;
And one said, "These are flowers that seek the skies,
  Loosed by the spell of their supreme desire."

# Philander's Song

*(From "The Sprightly Pilgrim")*

I sat and read Anacreon.
  Moved by the gay, delicious measure
I mused that lips were made for love,
  And love to charm a poet's leisure.

And as I mused a maid came by
  With something in her look that caught me.
Forgotten was Anacreon's line,
  But not the lesson he had taught me.

XI. Love Poems

## On the Upper Deck

*As the will of last year's wind,*
*As the drift of the morrow's rain,*
*As the goal of the falling star,*
*As the treason sinned in vain,*
*As the bow that shines and is gone,*
*As the night cry heard no more—*
*Is the way of the woman's meaning*
*Beyond man's eldest lore.*

### HE

This hour to me is like a rose just open,
The wonder of its golden heart not yet
Fully revealed.  So long I've waited for it,
Prefigured it in dream, and scourged my hope
With fear lest jealous fortune should deny,
That now I hardly dare—Am I awake?
Can it be true I have you here beside me?
Can it be true I have you here alone—
Most wonderfully alone among these strangers
Who seem to me like senseless shapes of air?
The throb of the great engines, the obscure
Hiss of the water past our speeding hull
Seem to enfold and press you closer to me.
No, do not move!  Alone although we be,
I dare not touch your hand; your gown's dear hem
I will not touch lest I should break my dream
And just an empty deck-chair mock my longing.
But (for the beggar may in dreams be king),
Oh, let your eyes but touch me, let my spirit
But drink, but drain, but bathe in their deep light,
And slake its cherished anguish.  Look at me!

### SHE

Look how the water's waiting holds the sky!
I think I never saw the Sound so still.
That wash of beryl green, that melting violet,
That fine rose-amber veiling deeps of glory
Our eyes could not endure—how each is doubled,
Lest we should miss some marvel of strange tone,
And be forever poor.  Such beauty seems
To cry like violins.  Hush, and you'll hear it.
Don't look at me when God is at his miracles.

[ 159 ]

He topped all miracle in making you.
Your mouth, your throat, your eyes, your hands, your
    hair—
To look at these is harps within my soul,
The music of the stars at Time's first morning.
How can I see the wide, familiar world
When all my being drowns in your deep eyes?
What is the maddest sunset to your eyes?
Let us not talk of sunsets.

SHE
           Soon this rose
Of incommunicable light will fade,
Its ultimate petals sinking in the sea.
Be still, and watch the vaster bloom unfold
Whose pollen is the dust of stars, whose petals
The tissue of strange tears, desire and sleep.

HE
We talk of roses, meaning all things fair
And rare and enigmatic; but the rose
Transcending all, the Rose of Life, is you!

*O Rose, blossom of wonder, dark blossom of ancient dream,*
*Wan tides of the Wandering Sorrow through your deep*
    *slumber stream;*
*Warm winds of the Wavering Passion are lost in your*
    *crimson fold,*
*And memory and foreboding at the hush of your heart lie*
    *cold.*

*O Rose, blossom of mystery, holding within your deeps*
*The hurt of a thousand vigils, the heal of a thousand sleeps,*
*There breathes upon your petals a power from the ends*
    *of earth.*
*Your beauty is heavy with knowledge of life and death*
    *and birth.*

*O Rose, blossom of longing—the faint suspense, and the*
    *fire,*
*The wistfulness of time, and the unassuaged desire,*
*The pity of tears on the pillow, the pang of tears unshed—*
*With these your spirit is weary, with these your beauty*
    *is fed.*

#### SHE

Woman or rose, your verses do her credit,
Barring some small confusion in the figure.

#### HE

'Tis fusion, not confusion.  So the rose
Be beautiful enough, and strange enough,
Love in his haste may take its sweet for you;
And sun and rain, wise gardeners, seeing you
With face uplift, will know the rose you are.

#### SHE

Let us not talk of roses.  Don't you think
The engines' pulse throbs louder now the light
Has gone?  The hiss of water past our hull
Is more mysterious, with a menace in it?
And that pale streak above the unseen land,
How ominous!  A sword has just such pallor!
(Yes, you may put the scarf around my shoulders.)
Never has life shown me the face of beauty
But near it I have seen the fear of fear.

#### HE

I knew not fear until I knew your beauty.

#### SHE

Let us not talk of me.  Look down, close in,
There where the night-black water breaks and seethes.
How its heart, torn and shuddering, burns to splendour!
What climbing lights!  What rapture of white fire!
Clear souls of flame returning to the infinite!

#### HE

If you should ever come to say "I love you,"
I think that even thus my life's dark tide
Would flame to sudden glory, and the gloom
Of long grief lift forever!  Dear, your eyes,
Your great eyes, shine upon me, soft as with tears.
Your shoulder touches me.  What does it mean?
I hold you to me.  Is it love—and life?

[ 161 ]

Let us not talk of—love! I know so little
Of love! I only know that life wears not
The face of beauty, but the face of fear.
The face of fear is gone. The face of beauty
Comes when you hold me so! Help me to live!
Help me to live, and hold me from the terror!

# A Nocturne of Consecration

I talked about you, Dear, the other night,
Having myself alone with my delight.
Alone with dreams and memories of you,
All the divine-houred summer stillness through
I talked of life, of love the always new,
Of tears, and joy,—yet only talked of you.

To the sweet air
That breathed upon my face
The spirit of lilies in a leafy place,
Your breath's caress, the lingering of your hair,
I said—"In all your wandering through the dusk,
Your waitings on the marriages of flowers
Through the long, intimate hours
When soul and sense, desire and love confer,
You must have known the best that God has made.
What do you know of her?"

Said the sweet air—
"Since I have touched her lips,
Bringing the consecration of her kiss,
Half passion and half prayer,
And all for you,
My various lore has suffered an eclipse.
I have forgot all else of sweet I knew."

To the wise earth,
Kind, and companionable, and dewy cool,
Fair beyond words to tell, as you are fair,
And cunning past compare
To leash all heaven in a windless pool,
I said—"The mysteries of death and birth
Are in your care.

You love, and sleep; you drain life to the lees;
And wonderful things you know.
Angels have visited you, and at your knees
Learned what I learn forever at her eyes,
The pain that still enhances Paradise.
You in your breast felt her first pulses stir;
And you have thrilled to the light touch of her feet,
Blindingly sweet.
Now make me wise with some new word of her."

Said the wise earth—
"She is not all my child.
But the wild spirit that rules her heart-beats wild
Is of diviner birth
And kin to the unknown light beyond my ken.
All I can give to her have I not given?
Strength to be glad, to suffer, and to know;
The sorcery that subdues the souls of men;
The beauty that is as the shadow of heaven;
The hunger of love
And unspeakable joy thereof.
And these are dear to her because of you.
You need no word of mine to make you wise
Who worship at her eyes
And find there life and love forever new!"

To the white stars,
Eternal and all-seeing,
In their wide home beyond the wells of being,
I said—"There is a little cloud that mars
The mystical perfection of her kiss.
Mine, mine, she is,
As far as lip to lip, and heart to heart,
And spirit to spirit when lips and hands must part,
Can make her mine.    But there is more than this,—
More, more of her to know.
For still her soul escapes me unaware,
To dwell in secret where I may not go.
Take, and uplift me.    Make me wholly hers."

Said the white stars, the heavenly ministers,—
"This life is brief, but it is only one.
Before to-morrow's sun
For one or both of you it may be done.
This love of yours is only just begun.

Will all the ecstasy that may be won
Before this life its little course has run
At all suffice
The love that agonizes in your eyes?
Therefore be wise.
Content you with the wonder of love that lies
Between her lips and underneath her eyes.
If more you should surprise,
What would be left to hope from Paradise?

So, Dear, I talked the long, divine night through,
And felt you in the chrismal balms of dew.
The thing then learned
Has ever since within my bosom burned—
One life is not enough for love of you.

## O Little Rose, O Dark Rose

O little rose, O dark rose,
With smouldering petals curled,
I am the wind that comes for you
From the other side of the world.

O little rose, O dark rose,
With the wild and golden heart,
I am your bee with burdened wings,
Too laden to depart.

O little rose, O dark rose,
Your soul a seed of fire,
I am the dew that dies in you,
In the flame of your desire.

O little rose, O dark rose,
The madness of your breath!
I am the moth to drain your sweet,
Even though the dregs be death.

O little rose, O dark rose,
When the garden day is done
I am the dusk that broods o'er you
Until the morrow's sun.

## A Nocturne of Spiritual Love

Sleep, sleep, imperious heart! Sleep, fair and undefiled!
 Sleep and be free.
Come in your dreams at last, comrade and queen and
  child,
 At last to me.

Come, for the honeysuckle calls you out of the night.
 Come, for the air
Calls with a tyrannous remembrance of delight,
 Passion, and prayer.

Sleep, sovereign heart! and now,—for dream and
  memory
 Endure no door,—
My spirit undenied goes where my feet, to thee,
 Have gone before.

A moonbeam or a breath, above thine eyes I bow,
 Silent, unseen,—
But not, ah, not unknown! thy spirit knows me now
 Where I have been.

Surely my long desire upon thy soul hath power.
 Surely for this
Thy sleep shall breathe thee forth, soul of the lily flower,
 Under my kiss.

Sleep, body wonderful. Wake, spirit wise and wild,
 White and divine.
Here is our heaven of dream, O dear and undefiled,
 All thine, all mine.

## In the Crowd

I walk the city square with thee.
 The night is loud; the pavements roar.
Their eddying mirth and misery
Encircle thee and me.

The street is full of lights and cries.
 The crowd but brings thee close to me.
I only hear thy low replies;
I only see thine eyes.

## A Nocturne of Trysting

Broods the hid glory in its sheath of gloom
Till strikes the destined hour, and bursts the bloom,
A rapture of white passion and perfume.

So the long day is like a bud
  That aches with coming bliss,
Till flowers in light the wondrous night
  That brings me to thy kiss.

Then, with a thousand sorrows forgotten in one hour,
  In thy pure eyes and at thy feet I find at last my
    goal;
And life and hope and joy seem but a faint prevision
  Of the flower that is thy body and the flame that is
    thy soul.


## Beside the Winter Sea

As one who sleeps, and hears across his dream
The cry of battles ended long ago,
Inland I hear the calling of the sea.
I hear its hollow voices, though between
My wind-worn dwelling and thy wave-worn strand
How many miles, how many mountains are!
And thou beside the winter sea alone
Art walking, with thy cloak about thy face.
Bleak, bleak the tide, and evening coming on;
And grey the pale, pale light that wans thy face.
Solemnly breaks the long wave at thy feet;
And sullenly in patches clings the snow
Upon the low, red rocks worn round with years.
I see thine eyes, I see their grave desire,
Unsatisfied and lonely as the sea's;—
Yet how unlike the wintry sea's despair!
For could my feet but follow thine, my hands
But reach for thy warm hands beneath thy cloak,
What summer joy would lighten in thy face,
What sunshine warm thine eyes, and thy sad mouth
Break to a dewy rose and laugh on mine!

# The Rose of Life

The Rose spoke in the garden:
"Why am I sad?
The vast of sky above me
Is blue and glad;
The hushed deep of my heart
Hath the sun's gold;
The dew slumbers till noon
In my petals' hold.
Beauty I have, and wisdom,
And love I know,
Yet cannot release my spirit
Of its strange woe."

Then a Wind, older than Time,
Wiser than Sleep,
Answered: "The whole world's sorrow
Is yours to keep.
Its dark descends upon you
At day's high noon;
Its pallor is whitening about you
From every moon;
The cries of a thousand lovers,
A thousand slain,
The tears of all the forgotten
Who kissed in vain,
And the journeying years that have vanished
Have left on you
The witness, each, of its pain,
Ancient yet new.
So many lives you have lived;
So many a star
Hath veered in the Signs to make you
The wonder you are!
And this is the price of your beauty:
Your wild soul is thronged
With the phantoms of joy unfulfilled
That beauty hath wronged;
With the pangs of all secret betrayals,
The ghosts of desire,
The bite of old flame, and the chill
Of the ashes of fire."

[ 167 ]

## Attar

The dark rose of your mouth
Is summer and the south to me;
The attar of desire and dream
Its tendernesses seem to me.

The clear deep of your eyes
A lure of wonder lies to me,
Whereto my longing soul descends
While love comes by and bends to me.

The hushed night of your hair
Breathes an enchanted air to me—
Strange heats from many a mystic clime
And far-off, perished time to me.

The pulses of your throat,
What madness they denote to me,—
Passion, and hunger, and despair,
And ecstasy, and prayer to me!

The dusk bloom of your flesh
Is as a magic mesh to me,
Wherein our spirits lie ensnared,
Your wild, wild beauty bared to me.


## Severance

The tide falls, and the night falls,
    And the wind blows in from the sea,
And the bell on the bar it calls and calls,
    And the wild hawk cries from his tree.

The late crane calls to his fellows gone
    In long flight over the sea,
And my heart with the crane flies on and on,
    Seeking its rest and thee.

O Love, the tide returns to the strand,
    And the crane flies back oversea,
But he brings not my heart from his far-off land
    For he brings not thee to me.

[ 168 ]

## The Hour of Most Desire

It is not in the day
That I desire you most,
Turning to seek your smile
For solace or for joy.

Nor is it in the dark,
When I toss restlessly,
Groping to find your face,
Half waking, half in dream.

It is not while I work—
When, to endear success,
Or rob defeat of pain,
I weary for your hands.

Nor while from work I rest,—
And rest is all unrest
For lack of your dear voice,
Your laughter, and your lips.

But every hour it is
That I desire you most—
Need you in all my life
And every breath I breathe.


## Spring Breaks in Foam

Spring breaks in foam
  Along the blackthorn bough.
Whitethroat and goldenwing
  Are mating now.
With green buds in the copse
  And gold bloom in the sun
Earth is one ecstasy
  Of life begun.
And in my heart
  Spring breaks in glad surprise
As the long frosts of the long years melt
  At your dear eyes.

[ 169 ]

## My Heart Is A House

My heart is a house, deep-walled and warm,
To cover you from the night of storm.

O little wild feet, too softly white
To roam the world's tempestuous night,
The years like sleet on my windows beat,—
Come in and be cherished, O little wild feet.
    For my heart is a house, deep-walled and warm,
    To cover you from the night of storm.

In the hillside hollow each lonely flower
Is closed against the disastrous hour.
The wet crow rocks in the wind-blown tree;
The tern drives in from the lashing sea.
    But my heart is a house, deep-walled and warm,
    To cover you from the night of storm.

Down from the naked heights of cloud
Care and despair cry low, cry loud.
The dark woods mutter with thronging fears;
The rocks are drenched with the rain of tears.
    But my heart is a house, deep-walled and warm,
    To cover you from the night of storm.

O little dark head, too dear and fair
For the buffeting skies and the bitter air,
Time sweeps the wold with his wings of dread,—
Come in and be comforted, little dark head.
    For my heart is a house, deep-walled and warm,
    To cover you from the night of storm.

## The Rose of My Desire

O wild, dark flower of woman,
Deep rose of my desire,
An eastern wizard made you
Of earth and stars and fire.

When the orange moon swung low
Over the camphor-trees,
By the silver shaft of the fountain
He wrought his mysteries.

The hot, sweet mould of the garden
He took from a secret place
To become your glimmering body
And the lure of your strange face.

From the swoon of the tropic heaven
He drew down star on star
And breathed them into your soul
That your soul might wander far—

On earth forever homeless
But intimate of the spheres,
A pang in your mystic laughter,
A portent in your tears.

From the night's heat, hushed, electric,
He summoned a shifting flame
And cherished it and blew on it
Till it burned into your name.

And he set the name in my heart
For an unextinguished fire,
O wild, dark flower of woman,
Deep rose of my desire.


## At Thy Voice My Heart

At thy voice my heart
    Wakes as a bird
Wakes in the night
    With sudden rapture stirred.

At thy look my soul
    Soars as a flame
Soars from the dark
    Toward heaven, whence it came.

At thy love my life
    Lifts from the clod
As a lily lifts
    From its dark sleep toward God.

[ 171 ]

## The Fear of Love

Oh, take me into the still places of your heart,
And hide me under the night of your deep hair;
For the fear of love is upon me;
I am afraid lest God should discover the wonderfulness
      of our love.

Shall I find life but to lose it?
Shall I stretch out my hands at last to joy
And take but the irremediable anguish?
For the cost of heaven is the fear of hell;
The terrible cost of love
Is the fear to be cast out therefrom.

Oh, touch me!   Oh, look upon me!
Look upon my spirit with your eyes
And touch me with the benediction of your hands!
Breathe upon me, breathe upon me,
And my soul shall live.
Kiss me with your mouth upon my mouth
And I shall be strong.

## Presence

Dawn like a lily lies upon the land
Since I have known the whiteness of your hand.
Dusk is more soft and more mysterious where
Breathes on my eyes the perfume of your hair.
Waves at your coming break in livelier blue;
And solemn woods are glad because of you.
Brooks of your laughter learn their liquid notes.
Birds to your voice attune their pleading throats.
Fields to your feet grow smoother and more green;
And happy blossoms tell where you have been.

# XII. Poems on Classical Themes

# Dedication of "Orion and Other Poems"

*To G. Goodridge Roberts*

These first-fruits, gathered by distant ways,
In brief, sweet moments of toilsome days,
  When the weary brain was a thought less weary
And the heart found strength for delight and praise,—

I bring them and proffer them to thee,
All blown and beaten by winds of the sea,
  Ripened beside the tide-vexed river,—
The broad, ship-laden Miramichi.

Even though on my lips no Theban bees
Alighted,—though harsh and ill-formed these,
  Of alien matters in distant regions
Wrought in the youth of the centuries,—

Yet of some worth in thine eyes be they,
For bare mine innermost heart they lay;
  And the old, firm love that I bring thee with them
Distance shall quench not, nor time betray.

*Fredericton, July, 1880.*


# Actaeon

### A Woman of Platæa Speaks

  I have lived long, and watched out many days,
And seen the showers fall and the light shine down
Equally on the vile and righteous head.
I have lived long, and served the gods, and drawn
Small joy and liberal sorrow,—scorned the gods,
And drawn no less my little meed of good,
Suffered my ill in no more grievous measure.
I have been glad—alas, my foolish people,
I have been glad with you! And ye are glad,
Seeing the gods in all things, praising them
In yon their lucid heaven, this green world,
The moving inexorable sea, and wide
Delight of noonday,—till in ignorance
Ye err, your feet transgress, and the bolt falls!
Ay, have I sung, and dreamed that they would hear;

[ 175 ]

And worshiped, and made offerings,—it may be
They heard, and did perceive, and were well pleased,—
A little music in their ears, perchance,
A grain more savour to their nostrils, sweet
Tho' scarce accounted of.   But when for me
The mists of Acheron have striven up,
And horror was shed round me; when my knees
Relaxed, my tongue clave speechless, they forgot.
And when my sharp cry cut the moveless night,
And days and nights my wailings clamoured up
And beat about their golden homes, perchance
They shut their ears.   No happy music this,
Eddying through their nectar cups and calm!
Then I cried out against them,—and died not;
And rose, and set me to my daily tasks.
So all day long, with bare, uplift right arm,
I drew out the strong thread from the carded wool,
Or wrought strange figures, lotus-buds, and serpents,
In purple on the himation's saffron fold;
Nor uttered praise with the slim-wristed girls
To any god, nor uttered any prayer,
Nor poured out bowls of wine and smooth bright oil,
Nor brake and gave small cakes of beaten meal
And honey, as this time, or such a god
Required; nor offered apples summer-flushed,
Scarlet pomegranates, poppy-bells, or doves.
All this with scorn, and waiting all day long,
And night long with dim fear, afraid of sleep,—
Seeing I took no hurt of all these things,
And seeing mine eyes were drièd of their tears
So that once more the light grew sweet for me,
Once more grew fair the fields and valley streams,
I thought with how small profit men take heed
To worship with bowed heads and suppliant hands
And sacrifice the everlasting gods,
Who take small thought of them to curse or bless,
Girt with their purples of perpetual peace!
Thus blindly deemed I of them,—yet—and yet—
Have late well learned their hate is swift as fire,
Be one so wretched as to encounter it;
Ay, have I seen a multitude of good deeds
Fly up in the pan like husks, like husks blown dry.
Hereafter let none question the high gods!
I questioned; but these watching eyes have seen

Actæon, thewed and sinewed like a god,
Godlike for sweet speech and great deeds, hurled down
To hideous death,—scarce suffered space to breathe
Ere the wild heart in his changed, quivering side
Burst with mad terror, and the stag's wide eyes
Stared one sick moment 'mid the dogs' hot jaws.

*　　*　　*　　*　　*

Cithæron, mother mount, set steadfastly
Deep in Bœotia, past the utmost roar
Of seas, beyond Corinthian waves withdrawn,
Girt with green vales awake with brooks or still,
Towers up mid lesser-browed Bœotian hills—
These couched like herds secure beneath its ken—
And watches earth's green corners.  At mid-noon
We of Platæa mark the sun make pause
Right over it, and top its crest with pride.
Men of Eleusis look toward north at dawn
To see the long white fleeces upward roll
Smitten aslant with saffron, fade like smoke,
And leave the grey-green dripping glens all bare,
The drenched slopes open sunward; slopes wherein
What gods, what godlike men to match with gods,
Have roamed, and grown up mighty, and waxed wise
Under the law of him whom gods and men
Reverence, and call Cheiron!  He, made wise
With knowledge of all wisdom, had made wise
Actæon, till there moved none cunninger
To drive with might the javelin forth, or bend
The corded ebony, save Leto's son.

But him the Centaur shall behold no more
With long stride making down the beechy glade,
Clear-eyed, with firm lips laughing,—at his heels
The clamour of his fifty deep-tongued hounds.
Him the wise Centaur shall behold no more.

I have lived long, and watched out many days,
And am well sick of watching.  Three days since,
I had gone out upon the slopes for herbs,
Snake-root, and subtle gums; and when the light
Fell slantwise through the upper glens, and missed
The sunk ravines, I came where all the hills
Circle the valley of Gargaphian streams.

[ 177 ]

Reach beyond reach all down the valley gleamed,—
Thick branches ringed them.  Scarce a bowshot past
My platan, thro' the woven leaves low-hung,
Trembling in meshes of the woven sun,
A yellow-sanded pool, shallow and clear,
Lay sparkling, brown about the further bank
From scarlet-berried ash-trees hanging over.
But suddenly the shallows brake awake
With laughter and light voices, and I saw
Where Artemis, white goddess incorrupt,
Bane of swift beasts, and deadly for straight shaft
Unswerving, from a coppice not far off
Came to the pool from the hither bank to bathe.
Amid her maiden company she moved,
Their cross-thonged yellow buskins scattered off,
Unloosed their knotted hair; and thus the pool
Received them stepping, shrinking, down to it.

Here they flocked white, and splashed the water-
    drops
On rounded breast and shoulder snowier
Than the washed clouds athwart the morning's blue,—
Fresher than river grasses which the herds
Pluck from the river in the burning noons.
Their tresses on the summer wind they flung.
And some a shining yellow fleece let fall
For the sun's envy; others with white hands
Lifted a glooming wealth of locks more dark
Than deepest wells, but purple in the sun.
And She, their mistress, of the heart unstormed,
Stood taller than they all, supreme, and still,
Perfectly fair like day, and crowned with hair
The colour of nipt beech-leaves:  Ay, such hair
Was mine in years when I was such as these.
I let it fall to cover me, or coiled
Its soft, thick coils about my throat and arms;
Its colour like nipt beech-leaves, tawny brown,
But in the sun a fountain of live gold.

Even as thus they played, and some lithe maids
Upreached white arms to grasp the berried ash,
And, plucking the bright bunches, shed them wide
By red ripe handfuls, not far off I saw
With long stride making down the beechy glade,

[ 178 ]

Clear-eyed, with firm lips laughing,—at his heels
The clamour of his fifty deep-tongued hounds,
Actæon. I beheld him not far off,
But unto bath and bathers hid from view,
Being beyond that mighty rock whereon
His wont was to lie stretched at dip of eve,
When frogs are loud amid the tall-plumed sedge
In marshy spots about Asopus' bank,—
Deeming his life was very sweet, his day
A pleasant one, the peopled breadths of earth
Most fair, and fair the shining tracts of sea;
Green solitudes, and broad low-lying plains
Made brown with frequent labours of men's hands,
And salt, blue, fruitless waters. But this mount,
Cithæron, bosomed deep in soundless hills,
Its fountained vales, its nights of starry calm,
Its high chill dawns, its long-drawn golden days,—
Was dearest to him. Here he dreamed high dreams,
And felt within his sinews strength to strive
Where strife was sorest, and to overcome;
And in his heart the thought to do great deeds,
With power in all ways to accomplish them.
For had not he done well to men, and done
Well to the gods? Therefore he stood secure.

But him,—for him—Ah that these eyes should see!—
Approached a sudden stumbling in his ways!
Not yet, not yet he knew a god's fierce wrath,
Nor wist of that swift vengeance lying in wait.

And now he came upon a slope of sward
Against the pool. With startled cry the maids
Shrank clamouring round their mistress, or made flight
To covert in the hazel thickets. She
Stirred not; but pitiless anger paled her eyes,
Intent with deadly purpose. He, amazed,
Stood with his head thrust forward, while his curls,
Sun-lit, lay glorious on his mighty neck,—
Let fall his bow and clanging spear, and gazed
Dilate with ecstasy; nor marked the dogs
Hush their deep tongues, draw close, and ring him
        round,
And fix upon him strange, red, hungry eyes,

And crouch to spring. This for a moment. Then
It seemed his strong knees faltered, and he sank.
Then I cried out,—for straight a shuddering stag
Sprang one wild leap over the dogs; but they
Fastened upon his flanks with a long yell,
And reached his throat; and that proud head went
     down
Beneath their wet, red fangs and reeking jaws.

    I have lived long and watched out many days,
Yet have not seen that aught is sweet save life,
Nor learned that life hath other end than death.
This horror like a cloud had veiled my sight,
That for a space I saw not, and my ears
Were shut from hearing; but when sense grew clear
Once more, I only saw the vacant pool
Unrippled,—only saw the dreadful sward,
Where dogs lay gorged, or moved in fretful search,
Questing uneasily; and some far up
The slope, and some at the low water's edge,
With snouts set high in air and straining throats
Uttered keen howls that smote the echoing hills.
They missed their master's form, nor understood
Where was the voice they loved, the hand that reared,—
And some lay watching by the spear and bow
Flung down.

          And now upon the homeless pack
And paling stream arose a stealthy wind
Out of the hollow west awhile, and stirred
The branches down the valley; then blew off
To eastward toward the long grey straits, and died
Into the dark, beyond the utmost verge.

# The Pipes of Pan

Ringed with the flocking of hills, within shepherding
    watch of Olympus,
Tempe, vale of the gods, lies in green quiet with-
    drawn,—
Tempe, vale of the gods, deep-couched amid woodland
    and woodland,
Threaded with amber of brooks, mirrored in azure of
    pools,
All day drowsed with the sun, charm-drunken with
    moonlight at midnight,
Walled from the world forever under a vapour of
    dreams,
Hid by the shadows of dreams, not found by the
    curious footstep,
Sacred and secret forever, Tempe, vale of the gods.

How, through the cleft of its bosom, goes sweetly the
    water Penëus!
How by Penëus the sward breaks into saffron and blue!
How the long slope-floored beech-glades mount to the
    wind-wakened uplands,
Where, through flame-berried ash, troop the hoofed
    Centaurs at morn!
Nowhere greens a copse but the eye-beams of Artemis
    pierce it.
Breathes no laurel her balm but Phœbus' fingers caress.
Springs no bed of wild blossom but limbs of dryad have
    pressed it.
Sparkle the nymphs, and the brooks chime with shy
    laughter and calls.

Here is a nook.  Two rivulets fall to mix with Penëus,
Loiter a space, and sleep, checked and choked by the
    reeds.
Long grass waves in the windless water, strown with
    the lote-leaf.
Twist thro' dripping soil great alder roots; and the air
Glooms with the dripping tangle of leaf-thick branches,
    and stillness
Keeps in the strange-coiled stems, ferns, and wet-
    loving weeds.

Hither comes Pan, to this pregnant earthy spot, when
  his piping
Flags; and his pipes outworn breaking and casting
  away,
Fits new reeds to his mouth with the weird earth-
  melody in them,
Piercing, alive with a life able to mix with the god's.
Then, as he blows, and the searching sequence delights
  him, the goat-feet
Furtive withdraw; and a bird stirs and flutes in the
  gloom,
Answering.  Float with the stream the outworn pipes,
  with a whisper,—
"What the god breathes on, the god never can wholly
  evade!"
God-breath lurks in each fragment forever.  Dispersed
  by Penëus
Wandering, caught in the ripples, wind-blown hither
  and yon,
Over the whole green earth and globe of sea they
  are scattered,
Coming to secret spots, where in a visible form
Comes not the god, though he come declared in his
  workings.  And mortals,
Straying at cool of morn, or bodeful hasting at eve,
Or in the depths of noonday plunged to shadiest
  coverts,
Spy them, and set to their lips; blow, and fling them
  away!

Ay, they fling them away,—but never wholly!  There-
  after
Creeps strange fire in their veins, murmur strange
  tongues in their brain,
Sweetly evasive; a secret madness takes them,—a
  charm-struck
Passion for woods and the wild, the solitude of the hills.
Therefore they fly the heedless throngs and traffic of
  cities,
Haunt mossed caverns, and wells bubbling ice-cool;
  and their souls
Gather a magical gleam of the secret of life, and the
  god's voice
Calls to them, not from afar, teaching them wonderful
  things.

# Marsyas

A little grey hill-glade, close-turfed, withdrawn
Beyond resort or heed of trafficking feet,
Ringed round with slim trunks of the mountain ash.
Through the slim trunks and scarlet bunches flash—
Beneath the clear chill glitterings of the dawn—
Far off, the crests, where down the rosy shore
The Pontic surges beat.
The plains lie dim below.  The thin airs wash
The circuit of the autumn-coloured hills,
And this high glade, whereon
The satyr pipes, who soon shall pipe no more.
He sits against the beech-tree's mighty bole,—
He leans, and with persuasive breathing fills
The happy shadows of the slant-set lawn.
The goat-feet fold beneath a gnarlèd root;
And sweet, and sweet the note that steals and thrills
From slender stops of that shy flute.
Then to the goat-feet comes the wide-eyed fawn
Hearkening; the rabbits fringe the glade, and lay
Their long ears to the sound;
In the pale boughs the partridge gather round,
And quaint hern from the sea-green river reeds;
The wild ram halts upon a rocky horn
O'erhanging; and, unmindful of his prey,
The leopard steals with narrowed lids to lay
His spotted length along the ground.
The thin airs wash, the thin clouds wander by,
And those hushed listeners move not.  All the morn
He pipes, soft-swaying, and with half-shut eye,
In rapt content of utterance,—
                              nor heeds
The young god standing in his branchy place,
The languor on his lips, and in his face,
Divinely inaccessible, the scorn.

# Passages from "Orion"

Two mighty arms of thunder-cloven rock
Stretched ever westward toward the setting sun,
And took into their ancient, scarred embrace
A laughing valley and a whispering bay.
The gods had stilled them in their primal throes,
And broken down their writhed extremities
Sheer to the open sea.  And now pine-belts
And strayed fir-copses lined their shaggy sides;
And inland toward the island's quiet heart
White torrents cleft the screens and answered each
To other from the high cliffs closer drawn,—
Kept ever brimming from eternal caves
In azure deeps of snow, and feeding full
A strong, swift river.  And the river flowed
With tumult, till it caught the mighty speech
Rolled upward from the ocean, when it paused,
And hushed its rapid song in reverence,
And wound slow-footed through the summer vale,
And met its sovereign with majestic calm.
The sunset with its red and purple banners
Hung softly o'er the bay, whose rippled breast
Flushed crimson; and the froth-streaks round the beach
Were glowing pink.  The sands burned ruddy gold,
And foot-marks crossing them lay sharp and black.
A flood of purple glory swept the shores,
And spread upon the vineyards and the groves
Of olives round the river-banks, and clothed
The further matted jungles; whence it climbed
The ragged scaurs and jagg'd ravines, until
It lay a splendour on the endless snow.

\*     \*     \*     \*     \*

    "With skins of lions, leopards, bears,
Lynxes and wolves, I come, O King, fulfilling
My pledge, and seeking the delayed fulfilling
Of some long hopes.  For now the mountain lairs
Are empty, and the valley folds secure.
The inland jungles shall be vexed no more
With muffled roarings through the clouded night
And heavy splashings in the misty pools.
The echo-peopled crags shall howl no more
With hungry yelpings 'mid the hoary firs.

The breeding ewe in the thicket shall not wake
With wolf's teeth at her throat, nor drinking bull
Bellow in vain beneath the leopard's paw.
Your maidens shall not fear to quit by night
Their cottages to meet their shepherd lads;
And these shall leave safe flocks, and have no need
Of blazing faggots. Nor without some toils
Are these things so. For mighty beasts did yield
Their ornament up most reluctantly;
And some did grievous battle. But the pledge
And surety of a blissful harbourage,
Whither through buffets rude I needs must fare,
Made heavy labours light. And if, hard pressed,
My knees perchance waxed faint, or mine eyes dim,
The strong earth stayed me, and the unbowed hills,
The wide air and the ever-joyous sun,
And free sea leaping up beneath the sun,—
All were to me for kindly ministrants,
And lent glad service to their last-born, man,
Whom, reverent, the gods, too, favoured well.
And if to me, sleepless, alone, by night
Came phantoms from polluted spots, and shades
Unfettered, wavering round my cliff-edged couch,
Fain to aghast me, them I heeded not,
As not worth heed. For there the deep-eyed Night
Looked down on me; unflagging voices called
From unpent waters falling; tireless wings
Of long winds bare me tongueless messages
From star-consulting, silent pinnacles;
And breadth, and depth, and stillness fathered me.

      *    *    *    *    *

And now it was about the set of sun,
And the west sea-line with its quivering rim
Had hid the sun-god's curls. A sanguine mist
Crept up, and to the Hunter's heavy eyes
Became as if his eyes were filled with blood.
He guessed the traitorous cup, and his great heart
Was hot, his throat was hot; but heavier grew
His head, and he sank back upon the sand,
Nor saw the light go out across the sea,
Nor heard the eagle scream among the crags,

[ 185 ]

Nor stealthy laughter echo up the shore,
Nor the slow ripple break about his feet.
The deep-eyed Night drew down to comfort him,
And lifted her great lids and mourned for him,
Foreknowing all his woe, and herself weak
To bend for him the indomitable fates;
And heavier dews wet all the trees and fields;
And sighs cool-drawn from infinite wells of space
Breathed round him; and from forth the unbowed hills
Came strength, and from the ocean essences
And influences to commune with him,
But found his spirit blind, and dumb, and deaf,
Not eager and expectant, as of old,
At every portal of the sleepless mind.
But hark! what feet are these that stir the vines
Beneath the big, sweet-smelling grape-clusters?
What feet are these that leave the muffling grass
And crush the shingle sharply up the beach?
Out of the foamless sea a heavy fog
Steamed up, rolled in on all the island shores,
But heavier, denser, like a cloak, where lay
The Hunter; and the darkness gathered thick,
More thick the fog and darkness where he lay,—
Like as a mother folds more close her child
At night when sudden street-brawl jars her dreams.

*　　*　　*　　*　　*

"We are all made heavy of heart, we weep with thee,
    sore with thy sorrow,—
The Sea to its uttermost part, the Night from the dusk
    to the morrow,
The unplumbed spaces of Air, the unharnessed might
    of the Wind,
The Sun that outshaketh his hair before his incoming,
    behind
His outgoing, and laughs, seeing all that is, or hath
    been, or shall be,
The unflagging Waters that fall from their well-heads
    soon to the sea,
The high Rocks barren at even, at morning clothed
    with the rime,
The strong Hills propping up heaven, made fast in
    their place for all time.

[ 186 ]

Withal the abiding Earth, the fruitful mother and
    kindly,
Who apportions plenty and dearth, nor withholds from
    the least thing blindly,
With suchlike pity would hide thy reverent eyes indeed
Wherewith the twin Aloïdes fain she would hide at
    their need.
But they withstood not Apollo, they brake through to
    Hades, o'erthrown;
But thee the high gods follow with favour, kind to
    their own;
For of thee they have not lacked vows, nor yellow
    honey, nor oil,
Nor the first fruit red on the boughs, nor white meal
    sifted with toil,
Nor gladdening wine, nor savour of thighs with the
    fat burned pure,—
Therefore now of their favour this ill thing shall not
    endure."

*    *    *    *    *

The cliffs are rent, and through the eternal chasm
A far-heard moan of many cataracts,
With nearer, ceaseless murmur of the pines,
Came with the east wind, whilst the herald gold
From cloven pinnacles on either hand
On gradual wings sank to that airy glen;
And many-echoed dash of many waves
Rose dimly from the cliff-base where they brake,
Far down, unseen; and the wide sea spread wan
In the pale dawn-tide, limitless, unportioned—
Aye sentinelled by these vast rocky brows
Defaced and stern with unforgotten fires.

*    *    *    *    *

Now Delos lay a great way off, and thither
They two rejoicing went across the sea.
And under their swift feet, which the wave kissed
But wet not,—for Poseidon willed it so,
Honouring his son,—and all along their way
Was spread a perfect calm.   And every being
Of beauty or of mirth left his abode
Under the populous flood and journeyed with them.

[ 187 ]

Out of their deep green caves the Nereids came
Again to do him honour; shining limbs
And shining bosoms, cleaving, waked the main
All into sapphire ripples, each where crowned
With yellow tresses streaming.    Triton came
And all his goodly company, with shells
Pink-whorled and purple, many-formed, and made
Tumultuous music.    Ocean's tawny floor
They all left vacant, empty every bower,
And solitary the remotest courts.
Following in the midst of the array
Their mistress, her white horses paced along
Over the unaccustomed element,
Submissive, with the wonted chariot
Pillowed in vapours silver, pink and gold,
Itself of pearl and fire.    And so they reached
Delos, and went together hand in hand
Up from the water and their company,
And the green wood received them out of sight.

www.ingramcontent.com/pod-product-compliance
Lightning Source LLC
Chambersburg PA
CBHW021142090426
42740CB00008B/906